WINE MAKING
WITH HERBS

by

IAN BALL

PAPERFRONTS
ELLIOT RIGHT WAY BOOKS
KINGSWOOD, SURREY, U.K.

Made and Printed in Great Britain by Hunt Barnard Printing Ltd, Aylesbury, Bucks.

WINE MAKING
WITH HERBS
IS
DEDICATED TO ERIN, WITH LOVE

Contents

1 Introduction

Easy-to-make herb wines and liqueurs soon reward us with an extensive range of delicious and inexpensive beverages to excite the senses. They appeal to our appetite for a full and long life, enriched by the superb natural herb goodness contained in unique and nourishing home-made herb wines and liqueurs.

All herb wines and liqueurs in this book can be made using fresh or dried herbs – readily available from herbalists, health-food stockists and some home-brew shops.

Herb wines and liqueurs have been made for centuries; their special therapeutic and healing properties are known to generations of country wine-makers. Many of the *secrets* of successful herb wine and liqueur making have remained jealously guarded – until now!

This book gives precise and simple to follow instructions to help you produce speedily a splendid selection of economical and luscious herb wines and liqueurs; brim-full with natural, health-giving ingredients. They will provide a tasty accompaniment to

7

mouth-watering meals; exciting parties; enjoyable social gatherings, and relaxed evenings at home.

Each recipe offers you the option of making fabulous full-bodied herb wine with pure fruit juice and/or grape juice and honey, *without adding sugar (sucrose) or chemicals*; or making delightful, especially economical though less full-bodied wine, using a necessary minimum of granulated sugar (sucrose) in place of grape juice and honey to ferment the alcohol content of your wine.

Whatever your preference in commercial wines, you'll quickly come to appreciate the fascinating array of eye-catching colours, heady herb-fragrances and lip-smacking savour of the original herb wine and liqueur recipes in this book, whose roots reach back into the golden age of antiquity.

Early history of herbs

The healing and health promoting powers of particular plants have been observed and recorded for several thousand years. Plants long credited with medicinal properties are called "herbs". Archaeological excavations indicate "primitive" man was aware of the beneficial and curative potential of herbs.

The Chinese were using herbal medicines in 3,000 BC! Ancient Egyptians employed herb doctors in 2,000 BC. Much of their knowledge was advanced upon by the ancient Greeks. The prestigious Medical School of Alexandria in Egypt, was a pre-eminent centre of learning – in 300 BC!

The Romans developed a considerable knowledge of herbs. Pliny the Elder (AD 23–79) wrote extensively on medicinal plants in his encyclopaedic work, *"Historia naturalis"* (Natural History). The Roman army planted herbs in occupied countries, and relied on the nutritional and medicinal value of herbs to keep soldiers strong, healthy and fighting-fit.

Pedanius Dioscorides (AD 40–90), a Greek physician and pharmacologist, employed in the service of the Roman emperor Nero as an army surgeon, listed the medicinal properties of almost 600 plants in his classic work, *"De materia medica"*. This remained the foremost pharmacological text for over 1,600 years!

Herb wines
The inhabitants of vine growing countries mixed herbs with fermenting pressed grape juice to create refreshing, fragrant-radiant herb wines – for health and pleasure! Delicious herb wines were also made by macerating herbs for 7 days in matured, ready-to-drink wine.

In colder climates, where grape vines did not prosper, and ale (made from barley), mead (made from honey) and cider (made from apple juice) were the customary beverages, herbs were often added to the fermenting brew to impart their unique flavours and medicinal qualities to the finished product.

The rediscovery of forgotten and neglected ancient wisdom in Europe during the "Renaissance" (*revival* of learning) period of the fifteenth and sixteenth centuries, rekindled the quest for herbal medicines, elixirs, aphrodisiacs and potions. Pioneering research by alchemists and monks led to the sometimes complex blending of herbs and wine, distilled into spirit, that we now call "liqueurs".

Liqueurs
Today, we enjoy the luxury of expensive commercial liqueurs after sumptuous dinners. Liqueurs were originally developed as powerful medicines! Popular

liqueurs include: Absinthe (wormwood flowers and leaves, liquorice, fennel, angelica, anise); Alkermes (orange flowers); Amourette (violet flowers); Anisette (anise seeds); Bénédictine (secret blend of herbs and spices – formula perfected in 1510); Chartreuse (secret blend of Alpine herbs, also spices – formula perfected in 1607); Crème De Menthe (peppermint leaves); Crème De Violette (violet flowers); Curaçao (orange peel, cinnamon, Pernambuco bark, cloves); Danziger Goldwasser (secret blend of herbs, spices and specks of real gold leaf!); Frigola (thyme); Juniper Brandy (juniper berries); Kümmel (caraway seeds); Sloe Gin (sloes); Van Der Hum (secret blend of orange peel, orange flowers, herbs and spices) etc., etc.

2 Traditional medicinal value of herb wines

In the Western world, orthodox medicine's comparatively recent preoccupation with laboratory produced chemical-based remedies is fast coming a full circle, with the realisation that many natural plant-based herbal medicines often work as well as – sometimes better than – artificial, commercially mass-produced and mass-marketed, chemically concentrated products; some of which have been proven to promote unpleasant, even sinister, side-effects.

Wholesome *natural* herbal medicines have long been highly esteemed throughout Asia, especially in India and China – where herbal remedies are today used alongside selected Western medical practices to achieve occasionally remarkable results.

Herb wines were among man's first natural medicines, and have been made by countless generations of health-conscious country folk. The wine making process draws all the herb's beneficial nutritional and medicinal properties into the finished wine,

11

and presents the jubilant winemaker with a delicious and powerful package of natural herb wine goodness!

Popular modern commercial herb wines include French and Italian Vermouths (cinchona, sage, nutmeg, clove etc.), Dubonnet, and "health-promoting" tonic wines.

Herbs listed on the following pages have established and well documented uses as prime ingredients and flavourings in natural wines and liqueurs. A brief selection of the *traditional* medicinal values of each herb is included for your interest and information only. In many cases the traditional medicinal properties of the herbs remain scientifically unproven, and no special claims can be made for the curative potential of any herb wines or liqueurs.

Please consult a doctor (General Practitioner) if you are unwell, and ask if it's advisable to consume alcohol while taking any medication prescribed.

Have fun sampling gorgeous herb wines and liqueurs for their undeniably pleasurable and therapeutic qualities, and regard any curative effect as a welcome bonus!

And *please* be aware of the dangers of *excessive* imbibing. Drink sensibly, stay healthy and enjoy an active and long life. Cheers and good health!

A-Z Guide to traditional medicinal values of principal herbs used for natural wine and/or liqueur making.

Agrimony (*Agrimonia eupatoria*).
Parts used for wine: Leaves.
Traditional medicinal value of herb: Tonic; strengthens and tones muscles; eases sore throats. Purifies the blood. Diuretic.

Angelica *(Angelica archangelica)*.
Parts used for wine: Leaves, sometimes roots; *for liqueurs:* Seeds, stem, roots.
Traditional medicinal value of herb: Stimulant and tonic; remedy for anaemia, colds, coughs, sore throats, mouth ulcers, and indigestion. Calms nerves. Long believed to strengthen heart muscles and help prolong life. Beneficial in treatment of rheumatism.

Anise *(Pimpinella anisum)*.
Parts used for liqueur: Seeds (aniseed).
Traditional medicinal value of herb: Stimulant and tonic; used to ease bronchitis and asthma; cures indigestion, soothes stomachs.

Balm, also known as **Lemon Balm** *(Melissa officinalis)*.
Parts used for wine and liqueur: Leaves.
Traditional medicinal value of herb: Tonic. Calms and soothes nerves; helps cure colds. Reduces pain – relieves headaches; remedy for insomnia. Heart tonic. Assists digestion of food.

Burnet *(Poterium sanguisorba* or *Sanguisorba minor)*.
Parts used for wine: Leaves.
Traditional medicinal value of herb: Stimulant and tonic – revitalises, restores vigour. Soothes stomachs. Until recent times, commonly credited with the power to staunch or slow internal and external bleeding.

Caraway *(Carum carvi)*.
Parts used for liqueur: Seeds.
Traditional medicinal value of herb: Stimulates a jaded appetite, assists digestion. Remedy for stomach upsets. Calms nerves.

Chamomile, also spelled **camomile** *(Chamaemelum nobile,* also known as *Anthemis nobilis).*
Parts used for wine: Flowers.
Traditional medicinal value of herb: Stimulant – sharpens appetite; soothes stomachs, relieves indigestion; calms over-excited nerves. Body tonic – strengthens tissues. Natural antiseptic; remedy for headaches, colds and bronchitis. Encourages restful sleep and fortifies system for stressful day ahead.

Clover, Red *(Trifolium pratense).*
Parts used for wine: Flowers.
Traditional medicinal value of herb: Calms nerves, increases appetite, assists digestion and helps cure coughs. Purifies the blood. For many years popularly regarded as a remedy for cancerous growths.

Coltsfoot *(Tussilago farfara).*
Parts used for wine: Flowers.
Traditional medicinal value of herb: General tonic; rich in minerals and vitamin C. Relieves coughs, colds, catarrh, bronchitis and asthma; soothes upset stomachs.

Dandelion *(Taraxacum officinale).*
Parts used for wine: Flowers, leaves.
Traditional medicinal value of herb: Tonic. Rich in minerals and vitamins A, B, C. Blood purifier; improves skin complexion. Beneficial in treatment of anaemia; eases rheumatism. Relieves indigestion and stomach upsets; mild laxative and diuretic.

Elder *(Sambucus nigra).*
Parts used for wine and liqueur: Flowers, berries.
Traditional medicinal value of herb: Stimulant; helps prevent and cure colds, coughs and sore throats. Strengthens body against infection. Remedy for asthma, bronchitis and constipation. Reduces nerv-

ous tension. Diuretic. Berries rich in minerals and vitamins A, B, C.

Fennel *(Foeniculum vulgare).*
Parts used for wine and liqueur: Seeds.
Traditional medicinal value of herb: Stimulant. Sharpens appetite, soothes stomachs, assists digestion. Relieves depression; calms nerves. Remedy for anaemia. Diuretic.

Golden-rod *(Solidago virgaurea* and *Solidago odora).*
Parts used for wine: Leaves, flowers.
Traditional medicinal value of herb: Extremely pleasant pick-me-up tonic effect. Remedy for sore throats and mouth ulcers; assists digestion – relieves indigestion. Diuretic.

Hawthorn *(Crataegus monogyna).*
Parts used for wine and liqueur: Flowers, berries.
Traditional medicinal value of herb: Helps cleanse system; relieves stress, fatigue and nervous disorders; remedy for insomnia. Long credited as a powerful heart tonic – improves circulation.

Hop *(Humulus lupulus).*
Parts used for wine: Female flowers (hop cones).
Traditional medicinal value of herb: Sharpens appetite, assists digestion – effective tonic for convalescents. Sedative – relieves pain, calms nerves and induces sleep. Natural antiseptic – remedy for throat infections and mouth ulcers. Diuretic.

Juniper *(Juniperus communis).*
Parts used for liqueur: Berries.
Traditional medicinal value of herb: Tonic and natural antiseptic – berries contain vitamin C; strengthens body against infection. Sharpens appetite, assists digestion, soothes stomachs. Remedy for catarrh.

Beneficial in treatment of arthritis and rheumatism.
Diuretic.

Lavender *(Lavandula officinalis)*.
Parts used for liqueur: Flowers.
Traditional medicinal value of herb: Tonic and natural
antiseptic. Used in treatment of colds, bronchitis,
asthma and nervous tension. Calms and relaxes body
and mind. Encourages untroubled, restful sleep.

Lime, also known as **Linden** *(Tilia europaea* and other
trees of the Linden family *Tiliaceae)*.
Parts used for wine: Flowers.
Traditional medicinal value of herb: Combats colds
and sore throats; purges system – cleanses stomach,
kidneys and bladder. Relieves nervous tension and
headaches; encourages restful sleep; improves skin
complexion and hair-health.

Marigold *(Calendula officinalis)*.
Parts used for wine and liqueur: Flowers.
Traditional medicinal value of herb: Stimulant. High
in vitamin C. Cleanses the blood and purges body of
impurities. Remedy for colds and stomach upsets;
eases rheumatism. Diuretic.

Marjoram *(Origanum marjorana),* also known as
Sweet Marjoram *(Majorana hortensis)*.
Parts used for wine: Leaves.
Traditional medicinal value of herb: Stimulant and
tonic. Restores lost appetite, assists digestion –
soothes stomachs. Calms nervous anxiety. Remedy
for colds, coughs and headaches. Diuretic, mild laxative.

Meadowsweet *(Filipendula ulmaria)*.
Parts used for wine: Leaves, flowers.
Traditional medicinal value of herb: Remedy for

colds; reduces fever. Used in treatment of arthritis and rheumatism. Diuretic.

Mint *(Mentha genus, over 20 species)*.
Parts used for wine and liqueur: Leaves.
Traditional medicinal value of herb: Stimulant – refreshing and revitalising. Assists digestion, soothes stomachs; relieves indigestion. Calms nerves, eases pain. Clears head and alleviates headaches. Natural antiseptic; remedy for colds and chills, menstruation disorders, hiccups; long believed to strengthen heart muscles. Diuretic.

Nettle *(Urtica dioica)*.
Parts used for wine: Leaves.
Traditional medicinal value of herb: Tonic, rejuvenates. Rich in vitamin C, protein and minerals. Purifies the blood; assists digestion; cleanses stomach, kidneys and bladder. Reduces fever, relieves backaches. Beneficial in treatment of colds, asthma, anaemia and rheumatism. Mild laxative and diuretic.

Orange *(Citrus genus, several species)*.
Parts used for wine and liqueur: Flowers; pure juice of orange fruits (oranges) – see page 21; sometimes also orange peel.
Traditional medicinal value of herb: Flowers calm nerves and relax body, encourage restful sleep. Remedy for nervous excitability, hiccups, insomnia, coughs and indigestion. For medicinal value of pure orange juice, see page 21.

Parsley *(Petroselinum crispum* or *Petroselinum sativum)*.
Parts used for wine: Leaves.
Traditional medicinal value of herb: Stimulant and

tonic – purifies the blood. Natural antiseptic; remedy for coughs, anaemia, asthma, menstruation disorders. Reduces fever. Combats rheumatism and arthritis. Soothes stomachs, assists digestion. Helps prevent development of cancerous growths. Rich in minerals and vitamins A, B, C, E. Diuretic.

Rose (genus *Rosa,* family: *Rosaceae* – over 200 species!).
Parts used for wine and liqueur: Petals, hips (rose-hips).
Traditional medicinal value of herb: Petals relieve catarrh, soothe stomachs; heart tonic, *Rose-hips:* Tonic. Contain vitamins A, B, C, E. Prevent and help cure colds, coughs and sore throats. Reduce anxiety, calm and encourage restful sleep.

Rosemary *(Rosmarinus officinalis).*
Parts used for wine: Leaves, flowers.
Traditional medicinal value of herb: Stimulant and tonic. Strengthens and tones muscles. Sharpens appetite, assists digestion, soothes stomachs, calms nerves and induces sleep. Natural antiseptic. Remedy for colds, sore throats, headaches and menstrual pain. Beneficial in treatment of anaemia, arthritis and rheumatism. Heart tonic; stimulates mind – improves eyesight and memory. Diuretic.

Sage *(Salvia officinalis).*
Parts used for wine: Leaves.
Traditional medicinal value of herb: Stimulant and tonic – dispels depression and brightens outlook. Strengthens the blood; improves circulation and calms nerves. Natural antiseptic; remedy for bronchitis, colds, sore throats and mouth ulcers. Reduces fever. Highly valued in treatment of rheumatism.

Assists digestion. Long believed to rejuvenate, pre-
serve eyesight, stimulate hair growth and retention,
improve memory and prolong life. Popularly believed
considerably to increase the chance of a woman con-
ceiving.

Sloe, also known as **Blackthorn** *(Prunus spinosa).*
Parts used for wine and liqueur: Berries (sloes).
Traditional medicinal value of herb: Tonic. High vitamin C content. Fortifies the body, helps prevent
and cure colds, coughs and sore throats.

Thyme *(Thymus vulgaris).*
Parts used for wine and liqueur: Leaves, flowers.
Traditional medicinal value of herb: Tonic, recommended in cases of mental and physical fatigue. Calms
nerves, encourages restful sleep, prevents nightmares. Natural antiseptic – relieves colds, headaches
and indigestion. Valued in treatment of anaemia,
asthma, arthritis, rheumatism and menstrual disorders.

Violet, Sweet *(Viola odorata).*
Parts used for liqueur: Flowers.
Traditional medicinal value of herb: Stimulant. High
in vitamin C. Relieves coughs, colds, sore throats,
bronchitis and headaches. Reduces nervous anxiety
and encourages restful sleep. Also mild laxative and
diuretic. Once popularly believed to help stop the
spread of cancerous tumours.

Woodruff *(Galium odoratum,* also known as *Asperula
odorata).*
Parts used for wine: Leaves.
Traditional medicinal value of herb: Tonic – invigorat-
ing. Natural antiseptic – cleanses stomach, kidneys
and bladder. Sharpens appetite, assists digestion.

Calms and soothes nerves; relaxes body – remedy for insomnia. Diuretic.

Yarrow (*Achillea millefolium*).
Parts used for wine and liqueur: Leaves, flowers.
Traditional medicinal value of herb: Tonic; cleanses and strengthens system, improves circulation. Rapid cure for colds, also indigestion. Diuretic. Since ancient times believed to help staunch internal and external bleeding.

Pure juices and honeys
Traditional herb wine and liqueur recipes are enriched by the addition of selected pure fruit and/or grape juices and honeys, specially chosen to complement and balance the flavour of the principal herb ingredient.

The nutritional and medicinal attributes of pure juices and honeys used, bestow their unique bounties in the ready-to-drink end product.

Nutritional and traditional medicinal value of pure juices and honeys used in herb wines and liqueurs.

● Pure juices and honeys are available from your local health-food stockist.

● *Pure apple juice:* Rich in vitamins A, B, C and minerals – calcium, iron, phosphorous and potassium. Pure apple juice fortifies the blood and tones the system. Improves skin complexion, clears up acne; eases catarrh; relieves emotional tension and headaches; assists digestion. Apple juice is a liquid food, which greatly benefits general health and increases vigour.

● *Pure grape juice (red or white):* Known to ancient peoples as "nectar of the gods". Rich in vitamins A,

B, C and minerals – calcium, iron and phosphorous. Highly nutritious, vitalising, body-building liquid food, it purifies the blood and cleanses the system. Valuable in treatment of anaemia, rheumatism, skin disorders, asthma, sore throats, catarrh and constipation.

● *Pure orange juice:* High in vitamins A, B, C and minerals – calcium, iron, phosphorous and potassium. Cleanses the system of impurities. Beneficial in cases of asthma, bronchitis and rheumatism.

● *Pure pineapple juice:* High in vitamins A, B, C and minerals – calcium, iron, phosphorous and potassium. Fortifies the body against infection. Assists digestion and helps remedy arthritis, catarrh and constipation.

● *Pure honeys:* Made by bees from the nectar of flowers, honey contains the nutritional and medicinal attributes of plants visited by the bees. Pure honey is rich in natural enzymes, minerals, proteins and vitamins B and C. Honey is a nutritious and easily digested high-energy food; it calms nerves, soothes the system; strengthens the blood, heart muscles and circulation. Honey vitalises and rejuvenates. Long credited as a natural aphrodisiac – stimulating sexual desire – raising and prolonging sexual performance; and it also is believed to increase a woman's fertility. Pure honey is used in the treatment of anaemia, arthritis, rheumatism, bronchitis, colds, coughs and sore throats. Honey is traditionally credited with the power to extend life expectancy and is a principal ingredient in some ancient formulas for *"The Elixir of Life"*.

3   The secret of sugar-free natural herb wine making

Delicious and easily made *natural* herb wine is produced by wine yeast *(Saccharomyces ellipsoideus)* converting natural sugar (fructose and glucose) present in dried grapes (sultanas or raisins), pure fruit juice and/or grape juice, and honey into alcohol.

Granulated sugar (sucrose) may be used as an economical replacement for grape juice and honey. Wine yeast also converts granulated sugar (sucrose) into alcohol.

Wine yeast's relatively speedy conversion of natural sugar (fructose and glucose) and any additional granulated sugar (sucrose) into alcohol is called *fermentation*.

For centuries country winemakers relied upon the natural sugar (fructose and glucose) present in fresh or dried fruit and fruit juice and/or grape juice plus honey, to supply the natural sugar (fructose and glucose) necessary for wine yeast to convert into the alcohol content of natural herb wines.

Refined sugar cane and sugar beet, familiar to us as processed household *granulated* sugar (sucrose), is not desirable in traditional *natural* herb wines.

Judicious blends of pure juices and honey (specially recommended because they complement the principal herb ingredient) with herbs and fresh or dried fruit – recipes in this book use sultanas *(dried white grapes)* or raisins *(dried black grapes)* – can replace the entire quantity of processed household sugar (sucrose) stipulated in many of today's versions of surviving and popular herb wine recipes.

List of equivalents
Approximate natural sugar (fructose and glucose) content of complementary ingredients recommended in natural herb wine recipes revealed in this book, together with approximate equivalent weight of processed household granulated sugar (sucrose).

Pure natural juices (available from your health-food stockist).

Pure apple juice – 1¾ pints (1 litre) contains the natural sugar (fructose and glucose) equivalent to about 4½ oz (127g) of granulated sugar (sucrose).

Pure grape juice (red or white) – 1¾ pints (1 litre) contains the natural sugar (fructose and glucose) equivalent to about 7 oz (198g) of granulated sugar (sucrose).

Pure orange juice – 1¾ pints (1 litre) contains the natural sugar (fructose and glucose) equivalent to about 4 oz (113g) of granulated sugar (sucrose).

Pure pineapple juice – 1¾ pints (1 litre) contains the natural sugar (fructose and glucose) equivalent to about 5 oz (142g) of granulated sugar (sucrose).

Pure honeys (available from your health-food stockist).

Pure honey – 1 lb (454g) contains the natural sugar (fructose and glucose) equivalent to about 14 oz (397g) of granulated sugar (sucrose).

Dried fruit

Sultanas (dried white grapes) and *raisins* (dried black grapes) – 12 oz (340g) of either contains the natural sugar (fructose and glucose) equivalent to about 8 oz (227g) of granulated sugar (sucrose).

Obviously the above equivalents can only be approximate. The precise amount of natural sugar (fructose and glucose) present in natural ingredients is likely to vary slightly from one season to another, and sometimes from one batch to another. However, the figures given are accurate enough for our purpose – to produce superb natural herb wines!

Wine making concentrated grape juice

Wine making concentrated white or red grape juice is available from home-brew stockists, and offers an economical alternative to *pure* grape juice. Recipes in this book give details for the optional use of wine making concentrated grape juice in place of *pure* grape juice recommended in the *"Sugar-free 'secret' recipe"* section of herb wine recipes. *Wine making concentrated white or red grape juice* – ¾ pint (426ml) contains the natural sugar (fructose and glucose) equivalent to about 12 oz (340g) of granulated sugar (sucrose).

Please be aware that wine making concentrated grape juice may include *chemical additives;* so check the label's contents list before you buy! Pure grape juice is your *natural* alternative.

4 Herbs

Herbs for making natural wines and liqueurs can be grown at home in your garden (some herbs also grow well indoors) or on an allotment. They can be used fresh, or bought as dried herbs from herbalists, health-food stockists and some home-brew shops.

Fresh herbs impart the best flavour and aroma to herb wines and liqueurs. However, *dried herbs* are quite satisfactory; convenient, easy and economical to use, and readily available to personal and postal shoppers throughout the year from commercial suppliers!

Growing herbs
Enjoy the bountiful and fragrant splendour of fresh herbs harvested from your own plants!

Herbs can be grown from seeds, young plants or cuttings. Everything you need to establish a splendid outdoors or indoors herb garden – including helpful books and brochures – is available from gardening shops and centres, nurseries and specialist herb farms.

Outdoors

Herb plants like a sunny, sheltered, south-facing position; with well-forked loose, adequately drained soil.

Herbs grow happily in small spaces – 2½ or 3½ square yards (2 or 3 square metres) can yield a plentiful supply of attractive and beneficial fresh herbs.

Plan the layout of your herb garden. Plant tall-growing herbs at the back, where they won't over-shadow smaller herbs. Keep *annuals* (lasting one season) and *biennials* (lasting two seasons) reasonably distant from *perennials* (last indefinitely) so the perennials' roots are not disturbed when replacing finished annuals or biennials.

Position the herbs to complement or contrast flowering colours; balance the overall display according to flowering times, and as you gain experience mix plants to blend their exotic aromas and sweet fragrances.

● Recipes in this book give a useful basic guide to each plant's approximate mature size, flowering time, colour, preferred soil type and favoured garden position.

Indoors

Some herbs grow well indoors, including 14 plants of special value to the maker of herb wines and liqueurs: angelica, balm, burnet, chamomile, dandelion, fennel, lavender, marjoram, mint, parsley, rosemary, sage, thyme and woodruff.

Herbs that grow well indoors can be cultivated in any suitable container – large pots, hanging baskets, tubs, troughs, window-boxes etc.

Indoor herbs like to be near light and sunshine, in a cool room – best not above 15°C (59°F); tucked away from draughts and safe from sudden changes in temperature.

Herbs living indoors flourish when cared for correctly; they need watering, feeding (with plant food) and occasional airing (open a window). A sprinkling of gravel over the soil surface prevents moss forming and retains moisture.

Do your homework before adopting herb plants; read about them and prepare their home properly. Love and cherish your herbs, and they'll bless you with gorgeous blooms and scents. Herbs reward our attention with their delicious flavours and beneficial properties; they delight us in health and help nurse us through illness.

Gathering herbs

A dry sunny morning in spring or summer is generally ideal for gathering leaves and flowers. Aim to collect herbs when they have developed abundant natural oils, flavour, colour and scent. Recipes in this book suggest best times to harvest herbs for making wines and liqueurs.

Pick leaves and flowers (in full bloom) after early morning dew has evaporated, and before strong sunshine volatises natural oils. Mid-morning is usually a good time to gather herbs but if you can't manage mornings, harvest in the cool early evening – before dew forms.

Finished flowers' *seed heads* (for seeds), and ripe berries are also best gathered mid-morning or early evening on a dry day.

☆   Golden Tips   ☆
Use strong scissors, a sharp knife or secateurs to snip stems when collecting leaves, flowers, berries or seed

heads. Avoid careless handling and bruising of herbs. Don't completely strip a thriving plant of leaves.

Fresh leaves or flowers soon wilt in plastic bags; they prefer a basket, big cloth bag or plastic *open* bucket. Berries like baskets and buckets. For seed heads use a large, strong paper bag.

Keep freshly gathered herbs safe from exposure to bright light or sunshine, which fades their colours; if necessary, loosely cover fresh-picked herbs with a clean dry cloth.

Wild herbs

Some herbs can be found growing wild. Before gathering wild herbs, check species are not rare locally or legally protected. Don't pick herbs likely to have been treated with chemical sprays, or growing near busy roadsides. Don't uproot wild plants, and please be certain you have correctly identified plants before picking (use a detailed, illustrated guide book).

Poisonous Wild Plants

Some herb-like wild plants are *poisonous*, including: Cowbane *(Cicuta virosa)*; Hemlock *(Conium maculatum)*; Fool's Parsley *(Aethusa cynapium)*; Fine-Leaved Water Dropwort *(Oenanthe aquatica)*; Hemlock Water Dropwort *(Oenanthe crocata)*; Parsley Water Dropwort *(Oenanthe lachenalii)*; and Tubular Water Dropwort *(Oenanthe fistulosa)*.

Also poisonous are: Bittersweet *(Solanum dulcamara)*; Black Bryony *(Tamus communis)*; White Bryony *(Bryonia dioica)*; Buttercup, all species *(Ranunculus)*; Foxglove *(Digitalis purpurea)*; Henbane *(Hyoscyamus niger)*; Lily Of The Valley *(Convallaria majalis)*; Meadow Saffron *(Colchicum autum-*

nale); Black Nightshade *(Solanum nigrum);* Deadly Nightshade *(Atropa bella-donna);* and Thorn-Apple *(Datura stramonium).*

Please note: The above *brief list* of poisonous wild plants is by no means exhaustive! Take great care to identify correctly wild plants used for making natural wines or liqueurs.

Preserving fresh herbs
   Herbs are best used fresh. However, good quality herb wines and liqueurs can be made from frozen or dried herbs. Surplus herbs harvested from bumper crops should be preserved for future use.
   To retain maximum natural herb oils, scent, flavour and colour, begin preserving freshly-picked herbs soon after gathering. You may like to wash the herbs gently in cold water to remove dust and insects; then *carefully* pat them dry between clean, soft cloth towels.

Freezing
   Some herbs freeze especially well, including: balm, berries of all types, burnet, marjoram, mint, parsley, rosemary, and thyme.
   Freeze herbs for wine or liqueur making whole or chopped, and unblanched. Store different herbs in separate containers; mark the contents clearly for quick and correct identification. Unblanched herbs should remain in good condition in your freezer for about 3 months; and berries for about 12 months.

Air drying
   Tie stems of fresh herbs in bunches, or put them in a fine-mesh bag, or spread them evenly on a clean paper-covered tray. Place the tray of herbs, or sus-

pend the herb bunches (upside down) or the fine-
mesh bag, in a warm, dry, airy situation; away from
strong light, smells (cooking, petrol etc.) and dust.
Suitable herb drying places include: an airing cupboard, a warm loft, a spare room, an understairs
cupboard, a non-smelly dry shed or a garage.

Herbs can take from 2 days to 3 weeks to become
crisp and brittle, ready for storing. The warmer your
drying place, the faster the herbs dry!

Oven drying

To oven-dry fresh herbs, spread herbs evenly on
a clean baking tray; place in an oven heated at a very
low setting to 35°C (95°F). Remove tray when the
herbs are crisp and brittle (usually 50–90 minutes).

Impatient winemakers can speed-dry herbs to crisp-
ness in 7–12 minutes; use an oven preheated to 110°C
(230°F, Gas Mark ¼).

Oven speed-dried herbs seldom produce the highest quality herb wines or liqueurs.

Seed heads

Harvest finished flowers' seed heads as the seeds
start to ripen (begin turning brown) and before the
seeds ripen fully and fall to the ground.

Drop the snipped off seed heads into a large, strong
paper bag or envelope 9 inches × 1 foot 1 inch
(230mm × 325mm). Make some small air holes
through the upper sides of bag or envelope – not
through the bottom! Then suspend the bag or
envelope in a warm, dry and airy place.

Occasionally shake the bag or envelope; the dried
seeds will fall to the bottom. Sieve the dried seeds
through a fine-mesh sieve or colander to separate the
seeds from the unwanted chaff. Wash the dried seeds
in a mug or small bowl of cold water, then strain

them and pat dry between clean, soft cloth towels. Place the seeds in a single layer on a clean paper-covered tray and put in a warm, airy place to dry thoroughly before storing.

Dried seeds, properly stored, keep in good condition for at least 2–3 years.

Storing dried herbs

Store dried herbs in airtight containers (jars, pots, tubs etc.), away from bright light, moisture, and heat. A normally dark or shaded cool position (cupboard, shelf, drawer, box etc.) is ideal.

Dried leaf and flower herbs stay in good condition for about 12 months.

☆ Storage Tips ☆

Clean, sterilise (see page 38), *rinse* and dry herb-storage containers before use. Label containers clearly with firmly glued labels; use an indelible ink (which won't run or fade) to write labels. Note the date herbs are stored. Periodically check filled containers to ensure herbs are not damp or mouldering.

Buying dried herbs

Dried herbs are easily and conveniently available to shoppers from herbalists, health-food stockists and some home-brew shops throughout the year!

Postal supply

A number of major herbalists offer postal supply of dried herbs from their extensive stocks, often by return post!

The up-to-date addresses of reliable postal suppliers are advertised in current editions of healthy living and health-food magazines, newsletters and some health and herb books.

Herbal teas

Herbal teas or "tisanes", give us an opportunity to sample the superb natural flavour of herbs, in a soothing cup of fragrant and delicious health-giving herbal tea!

All the herbs I recommend in this book for wine and/or liqueur making, brew delightful herbal tea. Use one heaped 5ml *tea*spoon of dried herb, or 3 heaped 5ml *tea*spoons of fresh (chopped and/or crushed) herb, to make one *strong* cup of herbal tea.

Brew herbal tea as you would ordinary (varieties of *Camellia sinensis*) loose tea leaves. Steep herb in a teapot of boiling hot water for 3–5 minutes; then strain the tea into a cup. If desired, sweeten to taste with pure honey, and savour the herbal nectar!

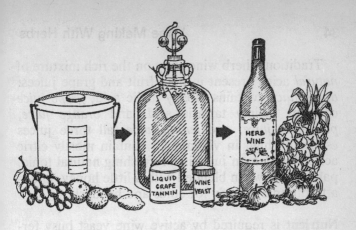

5 The alchemy of natural herb wine making

The highly complex, "magical" process by which water and pure fruit and/or grape juice is changed into wine fascinated medieval alchemists, and remains a challenge to modern vinologists, who study the science of wine making. The chains of natural chemical reactions occurring in fermenting and maturing wines can be difficult to analyse and sometimes defy precise duplication in laboratory controlled conditions. The skilled craft of natural wine making is an art which modern science cannot always guarantee to match!

Acid is an essential ingredient in wine. It acts as a natural antiseptic, destroying and inhibiting growth of hostile bacteria. Acid also encourages the rapid activity of wine yeast, adds flavour and zest to the fermented wine, helps wine keep and improve in storage, and assists development of the herb wine's delicate and appetising aroma.

Traditional herb wines rely on the rich mixture of *natural* acids present in pure fruit and grape juices: *apple juice* contains mostly malic acid; *grape juice* contains mainly tartaric acid; and *orange juice, pineapple juice,* and *lemon juice* (all three juices especially high in vitamin C) contain mostly citric acid. Pure lemon juice is a refreshing natural tonic, particularly when blended with a little honey, and is a traditional remedy for colds and headaches.

Nutrient is required by active wine yeast busy fermenting alcohol. Wine yeast thrives on vitamins B and C (supplied in natural juices) and minerals. *Sultanas* (dried white grapes) or *raisins* (dried black grapes) contribute extra vitamins A, B and a little C to natural herb wines; also minerals: calcium, iron, phosphorous, potassium; plus tannin and some tartaric acid.

Sultanas or raisins contribute "body" for wine yeast to cling on and work from. Wine yeast (a living organism) loves the presence of nutritious solid matter in the early stages (first 7–10 days) of fermentation, and responds to a vitamin and mineral boost with strong, accelerated and sustained performance in fermentation.

Tannin gives wine bite and character. It assists the natural acid to guard wine against bacterial infection and encourages newly fermented stored wine to clear quickly, ready for bottling. Tannin helps prevent oxidation (deterioration in the wine's quality following excessive exposure to air). Tannin – in moderation – promotes fast maturation and increases the wine's keeping qualities.

Natural tannin is present in many herbs (fresh or

dried), pure fruit juices and grape juices, sultanas and raisins. Tea leaves are a rich natural source of tannin.

Recipes in this book suggest the addition of cold, brewed tea as a tannin supplement to natural herb wines. Winemakers may choose to use winemaking dried tannin powder or liquid grape tannin, available from home-brew stockists, in place of the natural tannin present in cold, brewed tea. Follow the manufacturer's directions for use and remember to exclude the ½ cup of strong tea from herb wine ingredients.

Wine yeast *(Saccharomyces ellipsoideus)* is a fascinating life form. It is a plant, classified as a single-celled fungus; wine yeast's generic name – *Saccharomyces* – means "sugar fungus". Wine yeast lives and multiplies in sugary substances. Alcohol is a by-product of yeast's asexual and sexual reproduction!

Wine yeast lies dormant in extremely cold conditions. It multiplies increasingly quickly as the temperature rises. It ferments alcohol most satisfactorily in natural herb wines at a steady temperature of about 18°C (64°F), and normally cannot survive temperatures above 49°C (120°F).

The rising bubbles in fermenting wine result from the wine yeast's conversion of the wine ingredients' natural sugar (fructose and glucose) content, and any added processed household sugar (sucrose), into approximately equal weights of alcohol and harmless bubbling carbon dioxide gas.

When wine yeast has finished fermenting the natural sugar (fructose and glucose) and any additional processed sugar (sucrose) into alcohol, it ceases activity and settles dormant in the fermented wine's sediment.

Alchemical transmutation of natural herb wine
The correct blending of natural acids, herbs, nutrient, tannin, wine yeast and water (the origin and preserver of life) begins a unique act of creation. The separate natural ingredients combine, interact and transmute the liquids – water, pure fruit juice and/or grape juice, into ethyl alcohol *(aqua vitae* or "life water") and eventually matured natural herb wine. Down through the Ages it has been a symbol of youthfulness, vitality and long life.

Natural herb wines *are* "Elixirs of Life", and the modern winemaker shares the same thrill of creation enjoyed by the medieval alchemist!

6   Wine making equipment

To make 1 gallon (4½ litres) of wine, sufficient to fill six standard-size wine bottles, you need:

1. One 2¼ gallon (10 litre) plastic (food grade) bucket with close-fitting lid.

2. One 1 gallon (4½ litre) narrow-necked fermentation vessel. Specially designed winemaking fermentation jars or "demijohns" are available from home-brew stockists.

3. One bored cork or rubber bung and an air lock (air locks are sometimes called "fermentation locks").

4. One 1 gallon (4½ litre) storage vessel, in which to mature the fermented wine. Specially designed winemaking fermentation jars or "demijohns" are ideal for storage, and available from home-brew stockists.

5. One solid cork or rubber bung.

6. One 4 foot (1.2m) length of winemaker's plastic syphon tubing, and small plastic on/off tap.

7. Six standard-size wine bottles.

8. Six cork or plastic stoppers; or six standard straight-sided corks and hand corking machine (or lever-action corking machine), to drive the straight-sided corks down into the bottle necks.

Other items of value to the winemaker include: a large wooden or plastic spoon for stirring fermenting wine; a winemaker's fine-mesh plastic strainer or straining bag; a plastic funnel with a 5 inch (127mm) or 6 inch (152mm) diameter mouth; a plastic measuring jug (1¾ pints (1 litre) minimum capacity); accurate weighing-scales, and a bottle brush.

Useful optional extras include: a winemaker's hydrometer (see page 44) and trial jar and winemaking heating pad or belt to keep wine fermenting through the coldest weather.

Safety note: Never ferment wine in earthenware, enamelled or ordinary metal containers. Alcohol formed in fermenting wine might draw mildly poisonous chemicals from such containers into your wine. To be certain of safety, use fermentation vessels marketed for home wine making and brewing.

Stay in touch
Stay in touch with the latest developments in winemaking equipment and accessories. Visit your local home-brew stockist and view the articles on display; some items may prove a wise investment, saving time and effort.

The friendly specialist staff should be delighted to help you with advice and guidance on purchases, and wine making problems!

Sterilising equipment
Be certain your herb wines and liqueurs are not infected by bacteria on equipment. Sterilise all winemaking equipment and utensils before use.

Country winemakers traditionally relied on boiling water and/or oven baking to sterilise equipment, but these methods are not wholly adequate, and can be dangerous with glass items which might shatter!

Sulphite solution

For best all-round results use *sodium metabisulphite* (a powerful bacteria-killing chemical) in the form of a liquid "sulphite solution".

To make sulphite solution: Mix 1 oz (28g) of sodium metabisulphite powder, or 9 crushed Campden tablets (sodium metabisulphite in tablet form) in 1 pint (½ litre) of warm water.

Sodium metabisulphite powder and Campden tablets are sold by home-brew stockists, and some chemists.

Please note: Do not breathe the fumes given off when the chemical mixes with water. The fumes can cause momentary irritation to your nose, throat and lungs.

Store your sulphite solution in a clearly labelled, stoppered bottle. Rinse equipment and utensils with a sulphite solution before use. Simply pour the solution into cleaned buckets, fermentation and storage vessels, bottles etc.; swill the solution round, then pour it back into its bottle and re-stopper.

Always rinse away traces of sulphite solution from sterilised equipment and utensils with cold water before wine or liqueur making.

A mug, dish or small bowl of sulphite solution supplies a handy sterilising dip. To sterilise the outside of buckets, lids, bottles etc., dip a clean cloth in the sulphite solution and wipe the items. Do not forget to wash the cloth in cold water afterwards, then thoroughly rinse the sterilised equipment.

Sulphite solution is economical, it diminishes in quantity through usage, but remains potent for several months and may be used repeatedly!

Air locks

Pour a little sulphite solution into the air locks protecting the fermenting wine (see recipes). The solution has no contact with the wine, and destroys airborne bacteria which can – though seldom do – pass through a water-filled air lock and infect your wine.

Stains and moulds

To remove obstinate stains and moulds from fermentation vessels, bottles etc., soak them in warm water and washing-up liquid, or hot water and a few dissolved household soda crystals, or diluted or neat household bleach. Then scrub them clean with a winemaker's bottle brush, and rinse well with water.

Chemical *sterilising detergents,* that clean and sterilise in one operation, are available from homebrew stockists.

7 Notes on recipes

I've tried to make the following herb wine and liqueur recipes as self-contained as practicable. These notes are designed to give helpful hints and tips to supplement recipe instructions.*

Notes on the herb wine recipes follow; and notes on the herb liqueur recipes commence on page 50.

NOTES ON HERB WINE RECIPES
The unique herb wine recipes in this book make full use of natural chemicals, enzymes, vitamins and nutrients present in the wines' carefully balanced natural ingredients. Splendid herb wines can be made without resorting to artificial chemical additives.

Natural herb wines
Your natural herb wines should ferment, clear and mature to the highest degree of excellence *naturally*, without assistance from winemaker's artificial

*The technique of *natural* wine making is discussed more fully in this book's invaluable companion volume, "Wine Making The Natural Way"; published in the same series by *Paperfronts*.

chemical aids. However, these are *your* herb wines; please try winemaking chemicals *you think* might speed the wine making or maturation process. An impressive array of winemaking packaged chemical aids (supplied with full instructions) may be viewed on display at your local home-brew stockist.

Winemaking tannin

Herb wine recipes suggest the addition of ½ cup of cold, brewed tea as a tannin supplement to *natural* herb wines. You may prefer to use winemaking dried tannin powder or liquid grape tannin (available from home-brew stockists) in place of the natural tannin economically and conveniently supplied by cold, brewed tea. Winemakers choosing to use dried tannin powder or liquid grape tannin should follow the manufacturer's instructions, and remember to omit the ½ cup of strong tea from natural herb wine ingredients.

Honeys

Each herb wine recipe recommends a choice of pure honeys which are my personal favourites; selected because I believe they best complement the herb wine. Please experiment with *your* favourite pure honeys!

Wine yeast starter bottle

Wine yeast normally begins immediate activity once introduced, as instructed in recipes, to herb wine ingredients. To encourage a vigorous start to fermentation, prepare a wine yeast starter bottle about 48 hours before you commence wine making.

Method

Sterilise (see page 38) and *rinse:* one standard-size wine bottle, and plastic funnel. Place the funnel in the mouth of your bottle and measure into the funnel sufficient wine yeast to ferment 1 gallon (4½ litres) of wine – see the instructions supplied with wine yeast.

Pour into the bottle ¾ pint (426ml) of pure fruit juice, or pure grape juice from the total quantity of pure fruit juice or pure grape juice ingredient listed in the herb wine recipe you're following. You should count this ¾ pint (426ml) of pure juice as part of the total quantity of pure juice required to make the wine.

Plug the bottle mouth with a small wad of cotton wool, or cover the bottle with a 4 inch (102mm) square of sterilised, rinsed polythene – smoothed over the bottle mouth and secured around the neck with an elastic band, string or strong thread.

Keep the bottle in a warm place, around 24°C (75°F). The wine yeast multiplies in the pure juice, and after 48 hours should be active and ready to start fermenting your herb wine.

When the herb wine recipe instructs you to add the wine yeast, pour the fermenting pure juice from your wine yeast starter bottle into the plastic (food grade) bucket of prepared ingredients.

Vinegar fly
The vinegar fly *(Drosophila melanogaster)*, is attracted by the sweet scent of wine, particularly the fruity aroma of newly fermenting wine. Keep wine covered securely at all stages of its development, and mop up traces of spilled wine.

Wine the vinegar fly touches may be infected by bacteria which turn wine into vinegar!

Strength of herb flavour
The final strength of herb flavour in your matured ready-to-drink herb wine, is partly controlled by the number of days the fresh or dried herb is fermented

with other ingredients in your covered plastic (food grade) bucket.

My herb wine recipes suggest periods ranging from a minimum of 7 days to a maximum of 10 days.

Scooping and straining fermenting wine

Use a jug or mug to scoop fermenting wine from its sediment and strain through a winemaker's fine-mesh strainer or straining bag.

Wine hydrometer

Winemakers can use a wine hydrometer to measure the amount of natural sugar (fructose and glucose) and any added granulated sugar (sucrose) present in liquid being fermented into wine.

A hydrometer measures the *specific gravity* (relative density) of liquid. It is clearly marked with a scale of numbers, indicating a density of 1.000 kilogram per litre when floated in water. Sugars (fructose, glucose, sucrose) present in a liquid raise the level at which the wine hydrometer floats. The more sugars present in the liquid, the higher the figure indicated where the base of the curved surface of liquid (the meniscus) meets the hydrometer's number scale. This figure is called the *specific gravity*.

A winemaker's *hydrometer trial jar,* is the ideal vessel in which to float your wine hydrometer when measuring the specific gravity of a liquid, though any suitably deep – sterilised and rinsed – glass or plastic (food grade) vessel may be used. By locating the indicated specific gravity figure in a set of wine hydrometer tables, you can predict the approximate level of alcohol likely to be produced by the wine yeast's conversion to alcohol of all the sugars present in the liquid.

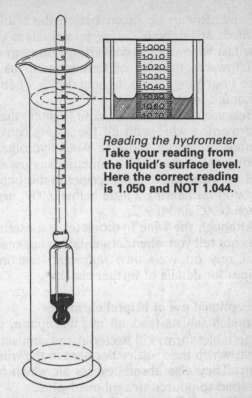

Reading the hydrometer
Take your reading from the liquid's surface level. Here the correct reading is 1.050 and NOT 1.044.

Many winemakers' hydrometers are marketed complete with tables and full instructions; here's an example of some readings:

Specific gravity	Sugars (fructose, glucose, sucrose) present in each gallon (4½ litres)	% Potential alcohol
1.010	3 oz (85g)	1%
1.035	15 oz (425g)	5%
1.070	1¾ lb (794g)	9%
1.105	2¾lb (1.25kg)	14%

Readings can be taken before the liquid is fermented; at intervals during fermentation (to check how fast wine yeast is converting sugars to alcohol), and towards the end of fermentation (as the raw wine's bubbling slows), to help decide when fermentation is complete.

Because alcohol is less dense (lighter) than water, a fermented wine with all the sugars converted to alcohol ordinarily shows a wine hydrometer final reading of less than 1.000; sometimes as low as 0.990.

Herb wines made using recipes in this book generally stop fermenting a little below 0.997, usually between 0.995 and 0.992.

Although the wine hydrometer is a useful tool, it does not tell you when fermentation has ceased; you must rely on *your own judgment*. See individual recipes for details of further checks.

The optional use of helpful chemicals

Campden tablets (sodium metabisulphite, see page 39, in tablet form) kill bacteria; and stun active wine yeast, which then settles dormant in the wine's sediment. They also absorb excess air which has been admitted to poured or syphoned wine.

The use of Campden tablets is *optional;* the addition of one crushed Campden tablet per gallon (4½ litres) of fermented wine about to be transferred to a storage vessel to clear and mature, speeds clearing.

One crushed Campden tablet per gallon (4½ litres) of wine may also be added before bottling, to absorb air and speed your wine's conditioning in the bottles.

Infection

In the unlikely event of your fermenting or maturing herb wine being infected by bacteria (surface film of white flecks developing etc.), one crushed Campden tablet added per gallon (4½ litres) of wine, immediately kills and/or inhibits growth of bacteria.

Where a crushed Campden tablet is added to newly fermenting wine, the wine yeast might be destroyed. To complete fermentation, add fresh wine yeast 24 hours after treating the infected wine.

Potassium sorbate (Sorbistat K) inhibits wine yeast from further activity in fermented wine, and may be added to fermented wine before storing the wine to clear and mature, or before bottling; follow the manufacturer's instructions for use.

Potassium sorbate may be used in addition to Campden tablets. However, its use is *entirely optional.*

Storage
Clearly label fermented wine stored to clear and mature before bottling (note on label date wine stored). Keep the wine somewhere cool – best below 15°C (59°F), dry and preferably dark; away from sunshine or strong light – which can fade the rich natural colour of herb wines, particularly red and rosé wines.

Clearing
Your herb wines should clear naturally within the recipe's recommended storage period. However, to quickly clear one gallon (4½ litres) of stubbornly hazy herb-wine naturally, simply pour or syphon 5 fl oz (142ml) of the hazy wine into a jug and whip in the *white* of one egg. Then pour the well-whipped mixture back into your storage vessel of hazy wine. Fit a cork or a rubber bung and keep in a cool place for 7–14 days to clear.

Bottling

Sterilise (see page 38) and *rinse* equipment and utensils before use. One gallon (4½ litres) of wine fills
six standard-size wine bottles. To prevent the rich
colour of red or rosé herb wines fading, use tinted
(not clear) wine bottles.

Straight-sided corks require a winemaker's hand
corking machine, or lever action corking machine, to
thrust them down inside the bottle necks.

Soften straight-sided corks before use by soaking
them for 24 hours in a sealed jar of sulphite solution
(see page 39). Cork or plastic stoppers don't need
softening or a corking machine as the stoppers are
pushed into place. Sterilise *cork* stoppers before use
by soaking them for 30 minutes in a sealed jar of
sulphite solution (see page 39); briefly submerge plastic stoppers. Rinse sterilised corks or stoppers in cold
water before use.

Safety note: Never fasten screw-caps on glass bottles
of herb wine. There is a chance that slight fermentation of any residual sugars may blow out corks and
stoppers; but screw-capped glass bottles could
explode!

To syphon

Use a 4 ft (1.2m) length of winemaker's plastic syphon
tubing, and an attachable small plastic on/off tap.
Place the vessel of wine on a sturdy, level surface
that is higher than the empty bottles to be filled.
Lower the syphon tube into your wine until it rests
just above the sediment at the vessel's base. Put a
plastic funnel in the neck of your first wine bottle.
Turn on the syphon tap and suck wine into the syphon
tube; direct the flow of wine along the funnel's mouth

into your bottle. Fill each wine bottle to within 2¼ inches (57mm) of its mouth.

When bottling is complete, fit stoppers or straight-sided corks. Then label bottles (note on the label the date the fermented wine was transferred to a storage vessel to clear and mature). Store bottles of herb wine somewhere cool, dry and away from sunshine or strong light.

Leave your herb wine to condition in bottles for at least 2 months before serving. Each herb wine recipe indicates when the wine achieves peak excellence.

To sweeten herb wine

To sweeten one standard-size bottle of dry (non-sweet) herb wine before serving, stir and dissolve one heaped *table*spoon of pure honey or caster sugar, in a *half* cupful of dry (non-sweet) wine poured from the bottle to be served. Warm the wine in a small saucepan for rapid dissolving. Mix the sweetened *cool* wine with the dry (non-sweet) wine by pouring the sweetened wine back into the bottle (use a plastic funnel), carafe or decanter.

Serving

For best results, chill bottles of herb white wine before serving; serve herb rosé wines cool, and herb red wines at room temperature. Gently pour the wine into wine glasses (tulip-shaped wine glasses are ideal). Fill each wine glass two-thirds full.

Aperitif wines (served before a meal) sharpen the appetite; table wines accompany and complement main meals, and social wines are eminently suitable for after-dinner evening enjoyment, cheese and wine parties, and light buffets.

Each herb wine recipe recommends the wine's suitability as an aperitif, table and/or social wine. Some herb wines are excellent all-rounders!

NOTES ON HERB LIQUEUR RECIPES

I hope you will find the detailed herb liqueur recipes easy to follow. Most of my herb liqueur recipes recommend the addition of small measures of spices; this advice reflects my own personal preference for modestly spiced liqueurs. Should you prefer *spice-free* beverages, then please exclude spices from your herb liqueurs. The superb herb liqueurs taste equally splendid with or without spices; simply follow my recipes, but miss out the spices.

Honeys
Each herb liqueur recipe recommends a choice of pure honeys to complement and enhance the liqueur's fabulous flavour; please feel free to experiment with *your* favourite pure honeys!

Straining
A winemaker's fine-mesh plastic strainer, or straining bag, is ideal for straining macerated herb liqueurs which are then ready for bottling and storage to clear and mature.

Filtering
Syphon or gently pour the liqueur from its sediment into a large jug. Cover the jug. Discard liqueur sediment left at the bottom of the bottle.

Winemaking circular *filter papers* of 6 inches (150mm) diameter, or preferably larger – around 9½ inches (240mm) diameter, are excellent for filtering your matured liqueur into a wine or liqueur bottle, ready for enjoyable drinking. Filter papers (use *coarse* grade for fast filtering) are available from home-brew stockists, chemists, and purveyors of laboratory equipment.

Method

Fold one sheet of circular filter paper in half, then fold in half again so the paper is quartered; then place the filter paper cone inside a sterilised (see page 38) and *rinsed* plastic funnel. The folds made in the filter paper fit it snug around the funnel's mouth.

Put the funnel into the neck of a clean, sterilised and *rinsed* empty wine or liqueur bottle, and fill the funnel with the liqueur up to the top edge of the filter paper. Leave the liqueur to filter slowly into your bottle; occasionally refill the funnel. The high alcohol content of the liqueur protects it from infection by airborne bacteria. Replace the filter paper if it becomes too clogged to filter the liqueur into the bottle.

Cotton wool

Cotton wool is an economical high-speed alternative to filter paper. Reasonably good, though less satisfactory, you can filter the liqueur through a small wad of clean cotton wool, plugged into the bottom of your funnel's mouth. Replace the cotton wool plug if it becomes too clogged to filter the liqueur into the bottle.

Serving

Most herb liqueurs are ready to enjoy 9 weeks after being bottled to clear and mature, and should continue to improve in quality for a further 9–12 weeks, before achieving peak excellence. Individual recipes give full information.

Liqueurs are traditionally served after evening dinner, in liqueur glasses at room temperature. Homemade herb liqueurs also make appetising aperitifs. Bon appétit!

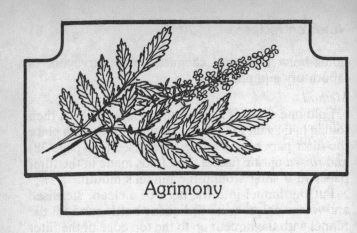

Agrimony

AGRIMONY *(Agrimonia eupatoria).*

Agrimony makes a popular traditional country wine and a herbal tea.

Agrimony is a perennial plant of around 2 feet (0.60m) in height. It likes well-drained soil in a sunny position and grows wild in grassy places. Agrimony's yellow flowers bloom from June to September.

Parts used for wine: Leaves (best gathered from flowering plants, June-August).

AGRIMONY HERB WINE

Agrimony herb wine develops a rich yellow-gold colour, with pleasing aroma and fruit-fresh taste; enjoyable as an aperitif, table or social wine of about 11.5% alcohol by volume.

Sultanas (dried white grapes) give extra flavour, body and smoothness to this wine and nourish the wine yeast, encouraging maximum efficiency in alcohol production.

*Dried herbs, pure juices and honeys are available from your local health-food stockist.

INGREDIENTS: to make 1 gallon (4½ litres).
Fresh agrimony leaves – ¾ pint (426ml)
   or *dried leaves – ¾ oz (21g)
Water – up to 1 gallon (4½ litres)
Granulated sugar – *(optional, see below)* **– 1½ lb**
   (680g)
Tea, strong – ½ cup
Sultanas – 12 oz (340g)
***Pure orange juice – 1¾ pints (1 litre)**
Wine yeast – amount recommended by manufacturer

SUGAR-FREE "SECRET" RECIPE (see page 23): To
make agrimony herb wine without adding sugar (sucrose) replace the entire quantity of granulated sugar
with **1 lb (454g) of *pure orange blossom or lime blossom honey; and either 2¾ pints (1½ litres) of *pure
white grape juice, or ¾ pint (426ml) of wine making
concentrated white grape juice.**

METHOD
   Sterilise (see page 38) and *rinse* wine making equipment and utensils before use. To measure fresh
agrimony leaves (if used – tear large leaves into
several pieces) gently press in measuring jug. Lightly
rinse fresh leaves in cold water. Put fresh leaves or
dried leaves in plastic (food grade) bucket. Cover.
Warm 1 pint (½ litre) of water in large saucepan. Stir
in granulated sugar or pure honey. When dissolved,
cover and leave to cool. Make tea, strain and allow
to cool, or use strained cold tea from an earlier brew.
Discard tea leaves or bag. Rinse sultanas in warm
water. Chop or mince sultanas. Pour pure orange
juice, and grape juice (if used), brewed tea, and dissolved sugar or honey into bucket. Add sultanas,
wine yeast and cold water to raise the total quantity

of liquid to about 7 pints (4 litres). Allow at least 2 inches (51mm) – 4 inches (102mm) at the top of your bucket for the fermentation's initial frothing. Cover. Keep bucket in a warm place for 7 days. Stir twice daily.

After seven days pour or scoop the fermenting wine from its sediment and strain into a narrow-necked 1 gallon (4½ litres) fermentation vessel. Discard solids. Top up to the neck with cold water. Fit cork or rubber bung and air lock filled with water, or sulphite solution (see page 39). Leave in the warm until fermentation is complete; this can take 4–5 weeks at an even temperature of 18°C (64°F).

Fermentation has finished when bubbles have ceased passing through the liquid in the air lock. A wine hydrometer reading (see page 44) of around 0.997 indicates fermentation may have ended. Check your agrimony herb wine tastes dry (non-sweet), is not fizzy on your tongue and is beginning to fall clear from the surface downwards.

When satisfied fermentation has finished, syphon or pour wine from its sediment into a narrow-necked one gallon (4½ litres) storage vessel. Top up to the neck with wine of a similar flavour and colour, or cold water. Fit cork or rubber bung. Store somewhere cool to clear and mature before bottling.

Your agrimony herb wine should be clear and ready to bottle after about 6 months' storage, though a few months longer improves the wine's quality. When bottled, the wine needs a further 2–3 months to condition and mature before drinking.

Agrimony herb wine achieves peak excellence about 20 months after the fermented wine has been transferred to a storage vessel to clear and mature.

Angelica

ANGELICA *(Angelica archangelica)*.

Oil from angelica seeds and/or roots is used to flavour many commercial liqueurs (including Chartreuse and Bénédictine; also gin and Vermouth), and in perfumes. Young stems and tender shoots make delicious candied sweetmeats, and the highly nutritious angelica plant can be prepared and eaten as a vegetable.

Angelica is a tall biennial plant of 5–6½ feet (1½–2 metres) in height. If left to flower, angelica can become perennial. It likes rich, moist soil in a shady position. Angelica's green-white flowers bloom from July to September.

● Angelica grows well indoors.

Parts used for wine: Leaves (best picked before the plant flowers), some traditional recipes use roots (best dug in autumn after the plant has finished flowering).

ANGELICA HERB WINE

Angelica herb wine develops a delicious smoky-honey colour, with a delicate aroma and full flavour; enjoyable as an aperitif, table or social wine of about 11.5% alcohol by volume.

Sultanas (dried white grapes) give extra flavour, body and smoothness to this wine and nourish the wine yeast, encouraging maximum efficiency in alcohol production.

*Dried herbs, pure juices and honeys are available from your local health-food stockist.

INGREDIENTS: to make 1 gallon (4½ litres)
Fresh angelica leaves – ¾ pint (426ml)
    or *dried leaves – ¾ oz (21g)
Water – up to 1 gallon (4½ litres)
Granulated sugar *(optional, see below)* **– 1½ lb (680g)**
Tea, strong – ½ cup
Sultanas – 12 oz (340g)
***Pure orange juice – 1¾ pints (1 litre)**
Wine yeast – amount recommended by manufacturer

SUGAR-FREE "SECRET" RECIPE (see page 23): To make angelica herb wine without adding sugar (sucrose) replace the entire quantity of granulated sugar with **1 lb (454g)** of ***pure orange blossom or acacia blossom honey; and either 2¾ pints (1½ litres) of *pure white grape juice, or ¾ pint (426ml) of wine making concentrated white grape juice.**

METHOD
Sterilise (see page 38) and *rinse* wine making equipment and utensils before use. To measure fresh angelica leaves (if used – tear large leaves into several pieces) gently press in measuring jug. Lightly rinse fresh leaves in cold water. Put fresh leaves or dried leaves in plastic (food grade) bucket. Cover. Warm 1 pint (½ litre) of water in large saucepan. Stir in granulated sugar or pure honey. When dissolved, cover and leave to cool. Make tea, strain and allow

to cool, or use strained cold tea from an earlier brew. Discard tea leaves or bag. Rinse sultanas in warm water. Chop or mince sultanas. Pour pure orange juice, and grape juice (if used), brewed tea, and dissolved sugar or honey into bucket. Add sultanas, wine yeast and cold water to raise the total quantity of liquid to about 7 pints (4 litres). Allow at least 2 inches (51mm) – 4 inches (102mm) at the top of your bucket for the fermentation's initial frothing. Cover. Keep bucket in a warm place for 7 days. Stir twice daily.

After seven days pour or scoop the fermenting wine from its sediment and strain into a narrow-necked 1 gallon (4½ litres) fermentation vessel. Discard solids. Top up to the neck with cold water. Fit cork or rubber bung and air lock filled with water, or sulphite solution (see page 39). Leave in the warm until fermentation is complete; this can take 4–5 weeks at an even temperature of 18°C (64°F).

Fermentation has finished when bubbles have ceased passing through the liquid in the air lock. A wine hydrometer reading (see page 44) of around 0.997 indicates fermentation may have ended. Check your angelica herb wine tastes dry (non-sweet), is not fizzy on your tongue and is beginning to fall clear from the surface downwards.

When satisfied fermentation has finished, syphon or pour wine from its sediment into a narrow-necked one gallon (4½ litres) storage vessel. Top up to the neck with wine of a similar flavour and colour, or cold water. Fit a cork or rubber bung. Store somewhere cool to clear and mature before bottling.

Your angelica herb wine should be clear and ready to bottle after about 6 months' storage, though a few months longer improves the wine's quality. When bottled, the wine needs a further 2–3 months to condition and mature before drinking.

Angelica herb wine achieves peak excellence about 20 months after the fermented wine has been transferred to a storage vessel to clear and mature.

LIQUEUR D'ANGÉLIQUE

Angelica liqueur is an exotic, revitalising beverage; a luscious green-yellow colour, with velvet-honey texture and exciting herb-spice taste. Alcoholic strength (when vodka or gin of around 40% Vol is used) about 23% alcohol by volume. Stronger spirit produces a more potent liqueur!

*Angelica candied stem, spices, pure juice and honeys are available from your local health-food stockist.

INGREDIENTS: to make 1 standard-size wine bottle.
*Pure pineapple juice – 6 fl oz (170ml)
*Pure lime blossom or mixed blossom honey –
   4 heaped tablespoons
Cinnamon (ground) – ¼ level 5ml teaspoon
Nutmeg (ground) – ¼ level 5ml teaspoon
Fresh angelica stem (cut while plant is flowering) –
   5 oz (142g)
   or *candied stem – 3 oz (85g)
Clove (whole) – 1
Vodka or gin – 17 fl oz (483ml)

Large jar (with tight-fitting lid) – big enough to hold all ingredients, or one empty 1 litre wine, spirit or cider bottle (in which to macerate ingredients) and cork or plastic stopper.

METHOD

Sterilise (see page 38) and *rinse* utensils before use. Warm pineapple juice in small saucepan. Stir in honey, cinnamon and nutmeg. When dissolved, cover and allow to cool. Rinse fresh angelica stem in cold water; slice fresh or candied angelica stem into thin pieces. Place angelica, clove, then vodka or gin and lastly juice-honey mixture in jar or bottle (use a plastic funnel for liquid). Fasten lid or stopper. Store somewhere warm for 10 days. Then strain liqueur through a fine-mesh strainer into a large jug. Squeeze liquid from angelica. Discard solids. Pour the cloudy liqueur through a plastic funnel into an empty wine bottle. Stopper the bottle with a cork or plastic stopper. Store in a cool place for 9 weeks to clear and permit the flavours to blend and mellow. Then syphon or carefully pour the liqueur from its sediment into a large jug; filter (see page 50) liqueur through a plastic funnel into an empty wine or liqueur bottle – fasten a cork or plastic stopper.

Your Liqueur D'Angélique is now ready to enjoy, and should continue to improve in quality for a further 9–12 weeks, before achieving peak excellence. Serve at room temperature in liqueur glasses. Good health!

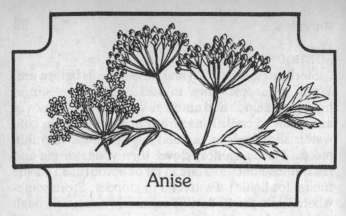

Anise

ANISE *(Pimpinella anisum)*.

Oil from anise seeds (aniseed) is used to flavour commercial liqueurs (including Absinthe, Anisette, Pernod, and Red Aniseed), and it is used in perfumes. Aniseed flavours confectionery – sweets, cakes, pastry, a German bread (Anisbrod), cheese and other delicious foods.

Anise is an annual plant of around 2½ feet (0.75m) in height. It likes light, dry soil in a warm, sunny position. Anise's yellow-white flowers bloom from July to August.

Parts used for liqueur: Seeds; harvest when ripe. Dry fresh seeds in a warm place (see page 30) before use.

LIQUEUR D'ANIS

Aniseed liqueur is a powerful yellow-gold beverage, with the gorgeous heady scent and smooth, appetising flavour of aniseed-liquorice. Alcoholic strength (when vodka or gin of around 40% Vol is used) about 23% alcohol by volume. Stronger spirit produces a more potent liqueur!

*Dried aniseed, liquorice root, spices, pure juice and honeys are available from your local health-food stockist.

INGREDIENTS: to make 1 standard-size wine bottle.
*Pure orange juice – 6 fl oz (170ml)
*Pure acacia blossom or mixed blossom honey –
    4 heaped tablespoons
Cinnamon (ground) – ¼ level 5ml teaspoon
Coriander (ground) – ½ level 5ml teaspoon
*Liquorice root, whole (dried) – 2 of average size –
    about 5″ (127mm) long and ¼″ (6mm) thick
*Aniseed (dried) – 1 oz (28g)
Vodka or gin – 17 fl oz (483ml)

Large jar (with tight-fitting lid) – big enough to hold
all ingredients, or one empty 1 litre wine, spirit or
cider bottle (in which to macerate ingredients) and
cork or plastic stopper.

METHOD
    Sterilise (see page 38) and *rinse* utensils before use.
Warm orange juice in small saucepan. Stir in honey,
cinnamon and coriander. When dissolved, cover and
allow to cool. Rinse liquorice root in warm water,
then break into ½ inch (13mm) pieces and crush with
rolling pin or hammer. Place aniseed, liquorice, then
vodka or gin and lastly juice-honey mixture in jar or
bottle (use a plastic funnel for liquid). Fasten lid or
stopper. Store somewhere warm for 10 days. Then
strain liqueur through a fine-mesh strainer into a large
jug. Squeeze liquid from soft seeds and liquorice root.
Discard solids. Pour the cloudy liqueur through a
plastic funnel into an empty wine bottle. Stopper the
bottle with a cork or plastic stopper. Store in a cool
place for 9 weeks to clear and permit the flavours to
blend and mellow. Then syphon or carefully pour the
liqueur from its sediment into a large jug; filter (see
page 50) liqueur through a plastic funnel into an

empty wine or liqueur bottle – fasten a cork or plastic stopper.

Your Liqueur D'Anis is now ready to enjoy, and should continue to improve in quality for a further 9–12 weeks, before achieving peak excellence. Serve at room temperature in liqueur glasses. Cheers!

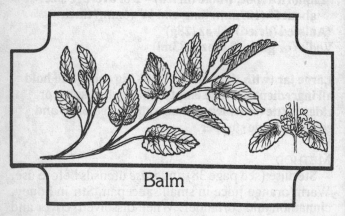

Balm

BALM, also known as LEMON BALM *(Melissa officinalis)*.

Oil from balm leaves is used to flavour commercial liqueurs, and it is used in perfumes. Balm leaves flavour fruit drinks, summer wine cups, salads, soups, stuffings and garnishings.

Balm is a perennial plant of around 2½ feet (0.75m) in height. It likes rich, moist soil in a sunny and sheltered position. Balm's white flowers bloom from July to September.

● Balm grows well indoors.

Parts used for wine and liqueur: Leaves (best picked early morning, before the sun is hot, from June to October).

BALM HERB WINE

Balm herb wine develops a honey-gold colour, with a sweet lemon fragrance and refreshing, full-flavoured taste; enjoyable as an aperitif, table or social wine of about 11.5% alcohol by volume.

Sultanas (dried white grapes) give extra flavour, body and smoothness to this wine and nourish the wine yeast, encouraging maximum efficiency in alcohol production.

*Dried herbs, pure juices and honeys are available from your local health-food stockist.

INGREDIENTS: to make 1 gallon (4½ litres).
Fresh balm leaves – 1 pint (½ litre)
    or *dried leaves – 1 oz (28g)
Water – up to 1 gallon (4½ litres)
Granulated sugar *(optional, see below)* **– 1½ lb (680g)**
Tea, strong – ½ cup
Sultanas – 12 oz (340g)
***Pure orange juice – 1¾ pints (1 litre)**
Wine yeast – amount recommended by manufacturer

SUGAR-FREE "SECRET" RECIPE (see page 23): To make balm herb wine without adding sugar (sucrose) replace the entire quantity of granulated sugar with **1 lb (454g) of *pure clover or mixed blossom honey; and either 2¾ pints (1½ litres) of *pure white grape juice, or ¾ pint (426ml) of wine making concentrated white grape juice.**

METHOD

Sterilise (see page 38) and *rinse* wine making equipment and utensils before use. To measure fresh balm leaves (if used), discard pieces of stalk and gently press leaves in measuring jug. Lightly rinse fresh leaves in cold water. Put fresh or dried leaves in plastic (food grade) bucket. Cover. Warm 1 pint (½ litre) of water in large saucepan. Stir in granulated sugar or pure honey. When dissolved, cover and leave to cool. Make tea, strain and allow to cool, or use strained cold tea from an earlier brew. Discard tea leaves or bag. Rinse sultanas in warm water. Chop or mince sultanas. Pour pure orange juice and grape juice (if used), brewed tea, and dissolved sugar or honey into bucket. Add sultanas, wine yeast and cold water to raise the total quantity of liquid to about 7 pints (4 litres). Allow at least 2 inches (51mm) – 4 inches (102mm) at the top of your bucket for the fermentation's initial frothing. Cover. Keep bucket in a warm place for 7 days. Stir twice daily.

After seven days pour or scoop the fermenting wine from its sediment and strain into a narrow-necked 1 gallon (4½ litres) fermentation vessel. Discard solids. Top up to the neck with cold water. Fit cork or rubber bung and air lock filled with water, or sulphite solution (see page 39). Leave in the warm until fermentation is complete; this can take 4–5 weeks at an even temperature of 18°C (64°F).

Fermentation has finished when bubbles have ceased passing through the liquid in the air lock. A wine hydrometer reading (see page 44) of around 0.997 indicates fermentation may have ended. Check your balm herb wine tastes dry (non-sweet), is not fizzy on your tongue and is beginning to fall clear from the surface downwards.

When satisfied fermentation has finished, syphon or pour wine from its sediment into a narrow-necked one gallon (4½ litres) storage vessel. Top up to the neck with wine of a similar flavour and colour, or cold water. Fit a cork or rubber bung. Store somewhere cool to clear and mature before bottling.

Your balm herb wine should be clear and ready to bottle after about 6 months' storage, though a few months longer improves the wine's quality. When bottled, the wine needs a further 2–3 months to condition and mature before drinking.

Balm herb wine achieves peak excellence about 20 months after the fermented wine has been transferred to a storage vessel to clear and mature.

BALM WHISKY LIQUEUR

Balm whisky liqueur is a bronze-gold colour, with a sweet, spicy aroma and smooth, fresh, soothing taste. Alcoholic strength (when whisky of around 40% Vol is used) about 23% alcohol by volume. Stronger whisky produces a more potent liqueur!

*Dried balm leaves, liquorice root, spices, pure juice and honeys are available from your local health-food stockist.

INGREDIENTS: to make 1 standard-size wine bottle.
Fresh balm leaves – ½ pint (284ml)
   or *dried leaves – ½ oz (14g)
***Pure white grape juice – 6 fl oz (170ml)**
***Pure orange blossom or acacia blossom honey –**
   4 heaped tablespoons
Cinnamon (ground) – ¼ level 5ml teaspoon
Nutmeg (ground) – ½ level 5ml teaspoon
Pure lemon juice – 2 level 5ml teaspoons
***Liquorice root, whole (dried) – 2 of average size**
   about 5″ (127mm) long and ¼″ (6mm) thick
Cloves (whole) – 2
Scotch Whisky or Irish Whiskey – 17 fl oz (483ml)

Large jar (with tight-fitting lid) – big enough to hold all ingredients, or one empty 1 litre wine, spirit or cider bottle (in which to macerate ingredients) and cork or plastic stopper.

METHOD

Sterilise (see page 38) and *rinse* utensils before use. To measure fresh balm leaves (if used), remove and discard pieces of stalk and gently press fresh leaves in measuring jug. Lightly rinse fresh balm leaves in cold water. Tear large leaves into several small pieces. Warm grape juice in small saucepan. Stir in honey, cinnamon, nutmeg and lemon juice. When dissolved, cover and allow to cool. Rinse liquorice root in warm water, then break into ½ inch (13mm) pieces and crush with rolling pin or hammer. Place balm leaves, liquorice, cloves, then whisky and lastly juice-honey mixture in jar or bottle (use a plastic funnel for liquid). Fasten lid or stopper. Store somewhere warm for 10 days. Then strain liqueur through a fine-mesh strainer into a large jug. Squeeze liquid from leaves and soft liquorice root. Discard solids. Pour the cloudy liqueur through a plastic funnel into an empty wine bottle. Stopper the bottle with a cork or plastic stopper. Store in a cool place for 9 weeks to clear and permit the flavours to blend and mellow. Then syphon or carefully pour the liqueur from its sediment into a large jug; filter (see page 50) liqueur through a plastic funnel into an empty wine or liqueur bottle – fasten a cork or plastic stopper.

Your Balm Whisky Liqueur is now ready to enjoy, and should continue to improve in quality for a further 9–12 weeks, before achieving peak excellence. Serve at room temperature in liqueur glasses. Cheers!

Burnet

BURNET *(Poterium sanguisorba or Sanguisorba minor)*.

Leaves of burnet ("salad burnet", "burnet saxifrage", "garden burnet") are popular country flavourings for butter, cream and cottage cheeses, salad, sandwiches, soup, stew and vegetables. Burnet leaves add zest to alcoholic and non-alcoholic beverages.

Burnet is a perennial plant of around 1 foot (0.30m) in height. It likes well-drained soil in a sunny position and grows wild in grassy places. Burnet's tiny green flowers – tinged deep red/purple – appear from May to August.

- Burnet grows well indoors.

Parts used for wine: Leaves (gather at any time from April to October).

BURNET ROSÉ

Burnet rosé develops an attractive orange-pink colour, with fragrant aroma and refreshing, soothing flavour; enjoyable as an aperitif, table or social wine of about 12.5% alcohol by volume.

Sultanas (dried white grapes) give extra flavour, body and smoothness to this wine and nourish the wine yeast, encouraging maximum efficiency in alcohol production.

*Dried herbs, pure juices and honeys are available from your local health-food stockist.

INGREDIENTS: to make 1 gallon (4½ litres).
Fresh burnet leaves – ¾ pint (426ml)
    or *dried leaves – ¾ oz (21g)
Water – up to 1 gallon (4½ litres)
Granulated sugar *(optional, see below)* **– 1½ lb (680g)**
Tea, strong – ½ cup
Sultanas – 12 oz (340g)
Lemons – 2
***Pure red grape juice – 1¾ pints (1 litre)**
Wine yeast – amount recommended by manufacturer

SUGAR-FREE "SECRET" RECIPE (see page 23): To make burnet rosé without adding sugar (sucrose) replace the entire quantity of granulated sugar with **1 lb (454g) of *pure orange blossom or mixed blossom honey; and either 2¾ pints (1½ litres) of *pure white grape juice, or ¾ pint (426ml) of wine making concentrated white grape juice.**

METHOD
Sterilise (see page 38) and *rinse* wine making equipment and utensils before use. To measure fresh burnet leaves (if used), discard pieces of stalk and gently press leaves in measuring jug. Lightly rinse fresh leaves in cold water. Put fresh or dried leaves in plastic (food grade) bucket. Cover. Warm 1 pint (½ litre) of water in large saucepan. Stir in granulated sugar or pure honey. When dissolved, cover and leave to cool. Make tea, strain and allow to cool, or use strained cold tea from an earlier brew. Discard tea leaves or bag. Rinse sultanas in warm water. Chop

or mince sultanas. Extract juice from lemons. Discard pips, pith and peel. Pour pure red grape juice and white grape juice (if used), lemon juice, brewed tea, and dissolved sugar or honey into bucket. Add sultanas, wine yeast and cold water to raise the total quantity of liquid to about 7 pints (4 litres). Allow at least 2 inches (51mm) – 4 inches (102mm) at the top of your bucket for the fermentation's initial frothing. Cover. Keep bucket in warm place for 7 days. Stir twice daily.

After seven days pour or scoop the fermenting wine from its sediment and strain into a narrow-necked 1 gallon (4½ litres) fermentation vessel. Discard solids. Top up to the neck with cold water. Fit cork or rubber bung and air lock filled with water, or sulphite solution (see page 39). Leave in the warm until fermentation is complete; this can take 4–5 weeks at an even temperature of 18°C (64°F).

Fermentation has finished when bubbles have ceased passing through the liquid in the air lock. A wine hydrometer reading (see page 44) of around 0.997 indicates fermentation may have ended. Check your burnet rosé tastes dry (non-sweet), is not fizzy on your tongue and is beginning to fall clear from the surface downwards.

When satisfied fermentation has finished, syphon or pour wine from its sediment into a narrow-necked one gallon (4½ litres) storage vessel. Top up to the neck with wine of a similar flavour and colour, or cold water. Fit a cork or rubber bung. Store somewhere cool to clear and mature before bottling.

Your burnet rosé should be clear and ready to bottle after about 6 months' storage, though a few months longer improves the wine's quality. When bottled, the wine needs a further 2–3 months to condition and mature before drinking.

Burnet rosé achieves peak excellence about 20 months after the fermented wine has been transferred to a storage vessel to clear and mature.

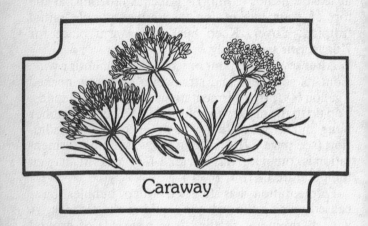

Caraway

CARAWAY *(Carum carvi).*

Oil from caraway seeds is used to flavour commercial liqueurs (including Aquavit, Bolskummel, and Kümmel), and it is in perfumes. Caraway seeds flavour bread, cakes ("seed-cake"), cheese and German *sauerkraut* (pickled cabbage). Several countries, including Denmark, The Netherlands and Poland, cultivate commercial crops of caraway.

Caraway is a biennial plant of around 2 feet (0.60m) in height. It likes well-drained soil in a sunny position. Caraway's white flowers bloom from June to July.

Parts used for liqueur: Seeds (harvest when ripe – dry in a warm place, see page 30).

KÜMMEL LIQUEUR

Kümmel (German for *caraway*) liqueur is a bright, honey-gold colour, with a warm, refreshing taste and delightful spicy aroma. Alcoholic strength (when brandy of around 40% Vol is used) about 23% alcohol by volume. Stronger brandy produces a more potent liqueur!

*Dried caraway seeds, spices, pure juice and honeys are available from your local health-food stockist.

INGREDIENTS: to make 1 standard-size wine bottle.
*Pure apple juice – 6 fl oz (170ml)
*Pure acacia blossom or mixed blossom honey –
   4 heaped tablespoons
Cinnamon (ground) – ¼ level 5ml teaspoon
Nutmeg (ground) – ¼ level 5ml teaspoon
Pure lemon juice – 2 level 5ml teaspoons
*Caraway seed (dried) – 1 oz (28g)
Cloves (whole) – 3
Brandy – 17 fl oz (483ml)

Large jar (with tight-fitting lid) – big enough to hold all ingredients, or one empty 1 litre wine, spirit or cider bottle (in which to macerate ingredients) and cork or plastic stopper.

METHOD

Sterilise (see page 38) and *rinse* utensils before use. Warm apple juice in small saucepan. Stir in honey, cinnamon, nutmeg and lemon juice. When dissolved, cover and allow to cool. Place caraway seeds, cloves, then brandy and lastly juice-honey mixture in jar or bottle (use a plastic funnel for liquid). Fasten lid or stopper. Store somewhere warm for 10 days. Then

strain liqueur through a fine-mesh strainer into a large
jug. Discard solids. Pour the cloudy liqueur through
a plastic funnel into an empty wine bottle. Stopper
the bottle with a cork or plastic stopper. Store in a
cool place for 9 weeks to clear and permit the flavours
to blend and mellow. Then syphon or carefully pour
the liqueur from its sediment into a large jug; filter
(see page 50) liqueur through a plastic funnel into an
empty wine or liqueur bottle – fasten a cork or plastic
stopper.

Your Kümmel Liqueur is now ready to enjoy, and
should continue to improve in quality for a further
9–12 weeks, before achieving peak excellence. Serve
at room temperature in liqueur glasses. Good health!

Chamomile

CHAMOMILE, also spelled CAMOMILE *(Chamaemelum nobile,* also known as *Anthemis nobilis).*

Chamomile has been valued as a medicinal plant
for over 2,500 years. The ancient Egyptians and
Greeks recorded their praise for "noble" chamomile.

The sweet-scented flowers make an excellent natural shampoo, beauty lotion (to improve skin complexion) and herbal bath salts.

In the Tudor England of King Henry VIII (1491–1547) and Queen Elizabeth I (1533–1603) chamomile *lawns* were planted by wealthy courtiers. A beautiful, fragrant and hard-wearing chamomile lawn is far more attractive and serviceable than modern grass lawns!

Chamomile flowers flavour popular traditional country wine, ale and herbal tea.

Chamomile is a perennial, evergreen ground cover plant of around 6 inches (0.15m) in height. It likes well-drained soil in a sunny position. Chamomile's white, daisy-like flowers, bloom from June to August.

● Chamomile grows well indoors.

Parts used for wine: Flowers (flower heads) – harvest at any time during the plant's flowering period; best picked on the morning of a bright day.

CHAMOMILE FLOWER HERB WINE

Chamomile flower herb wine develops a light honey-gold colour, with sweet fragrance and delicious fruit-flower flavour; enjoyable as an aperitif, table or social wine of about 11.5% alcohol by volume.

Sultanas (dried white grapes) give extra flavour, body and smoothness to this wine and nourish the wine yeast, encouraging maximum efficiency in alcohol production.

*Dried herbs, pure juices and honeys are available from your local health-food stockist.

INGREDIENTS: to make 1 gallon (4½ litres).
Fresh chamomile flower heads – ¾ pint (426ml)
   or *dried heads – ¾ oz (21g)
Water – up to 1 gallon (4½ litres)
Granulated sugar *(optional, see below)* **– 1½ lb (680g)**
Tea, strong – ½ cup
Sultanas – 12 oz (340g)
Lemons – 2
*Pure apple juice – 1¾ pints (1 litre)
Wine yeast – amount recommended by manufacturer

SUGAR-FREE "SECRET" RECIPE (see page 23): To make chamomile flower herb wine without adding sugar (sucrose) replace the entire quantity of granulated sugar with **1 lb (454g) of *pure lime blossom or acacia blossom honey; and either 2¾ pints (1½ litres) of *pure white grape juice, or ¾ pint (426ml) of wine making concentrated white grape juice.**

METHOD
Sterilise (see page 38) and *rinse* wine making equipment and utensils before use. To measure fresh chamomile heads (if used), discard pieces of stalk and gently press heads in measuring jug. Lightly rinse fresh heads in cold water. Put fresh or dried heads in plastic (food grade) bucket. Cover. Warm 1 pint (½ litre) of water in large saucepan. Stir in granulated sugar or pure honey. When dissolved, cover and leave to cool. Make tea, strain and allow to cool, or use strained cold tea from an earlier brew. Discard tea leaves or bag. Rinse sultanas in warm water. Chop or mince sultanas. Extract juice from lemons. Discard pips, pith and peel. Pour pure apple juice and white grape juice (if used), lemon juice, brewed tea, and dissolved sugar or honey into bucket. Add sultanas, wine yeast and cold water to raise the total quantity

of liquid to about 7 pints (4 litres). Allow at least 2 inches (51mm) – 4 inches (102mm) at the top of your bucket for the fermentation's initial frothing. Cover. Keep bucket in a warm place for 7 days. Stir twice daily.

After seven days pour or scoop the fermenting wine from its sediment and strain into a narrow-necked 1 gallon (4½ litres) fermentation vessel. Discard solids. Top up to the neck with cold water. Fit cork or rubber bung and air lock filled with water, or sulphite solution (see page 39). Leave in the warm until fermentation is complete; this can take 4–5 weeks at an even temperature of 18°C (64°F).

Fermentation has finished when bubbles have ceased passing through the liquid in the air lock. A wine hydrometer reading (see page 44) of around 0.997 indicates fermentation may have ended. Check your chamomile flower herb wine tastes dry (non-sweet), is not fizzy on your tongue and is beginning to fall clear from the surface downwards.

When satisfied fermentation has finished, syphon or pour wine from its sediment into a narrow-necked one gallon (4½ litres) storage vessel. Top up to the neck with wine of a similar flavour and colour, or cold water. Fit a cork or rubber bung. Store somewhere cool to clear and mature before bottling.

Your chamomile flower herb wine should be clear and ready to bottle after about 6 months' storage, though a few months longer improves the wine's quality. When bottled, the wine needs a further 2–3 months to condition and mature before drinking.

Chamomile flower herb wine achieves peak excellence about 18 months after the fermented wine has been transferred to a storage vessel to clear and mature.

Red Clover

CLOVER, RED *(Trifolium pratense).*

Red clover, which is high in protein and minerals, is valued by farmers as a source of nourishment for livestock. Red clover flowers make a delicious rosé wine.

Red clover is a short-lived perennial, often classed as a biennial, of around 10 inches (0.25m) in height. It likes fertile soil in a sunny position; grows wild in grassy places and looks good in gardens. Red clover's pink-purple flowers bloom from June to August.

Parts used for wine: Flowers (best picked while in full bloom – before noon on a sunny day).

RED CLOVER FLOWER ROSÉ

Red clover flower rosé develops a beautiful pink-rosé colour, with sweet fragrance and delicious taste; enjoyable as an aperitif, table or social wine of about 12.5% alcohol by volume.

Sultanas (dried white grapes) give extra flavour, body and smoothness to this wine and nourish the wine yeast, encouraging maximum efficiency in alcohol production.

*Dried herbs, pure juices and honeys are available from your local health-food stockist. Dried red clover flowers are also available from home-brew stockists.

INGREDIENTS: to make 1 gallon (4½ litres).
Fresh red clover flower heads – 1¾ pints (1 litre)
   or *dried heads – 2 oz (56g)
Water – up to 1 gallon (4½ litres)
Granulated sugar *(optional, see below)* **– 1½ lb (680g)**
Tea, strong – ½ cup
Sultanas – 12 oz (340g)
Lemons – 2
*Pure red grape juice – 1¾ pints (1 litre)
Wine yeast – amount recommended by manufacturer

SUGAR-FREE "SECRET" RECIPE (see page 23): To make red clover flower rosé without adding sugar (sucrose) replace the entire quantity of granulated sugar with **1 lb (454g) of *pure clover or acacia blossom honey**; and either **2¾ pints (1½ litres) of *pure white grape juice**, or **¾ pint (426ml) of wine making concentrated white grape juice**.

METHOD
Sterilise (see page 38) and *rinse* wine making equipment and utensils before use. To measure fresh clover flower heads (if used), remove and discard pieces of green leaf and stalk and gently press heads in measuring jug. Lightly rinse fresh heads in cold water. Put fresh or dried heads in plastic (food grade) bucket. Cover. Warm 1 pint (½ litre) of water in large saucepan. Stir in granulated sugar or pure honey. When dissolved, cover and leave to cool. Make tea, strain and allow to cool, or use strained cold tea from an earlier brew. Discard tea leaves or bag. Rinse sultanas in warm water. Chop or mince sultanas. Extract juice

from lemons. Discard pips, pith and peel. Pour pure red grape juice and white grape juice (if used), lemon juice, brewed tea, and dissolved sugar or honey into bucket. Add sultanas, wine yeast and cold water to raise the total quantity of liquid to about 7 pints (4 litres). Allow at least 2 inches (51mm) – 4 inches (102mm) at the top of your bucket for the fermentation's initial frothing. Cover. Keep bucket in a warm place for 9 days. Stir twice daily.

After nine days pour or scoop the fermenting wine from its sediment and strain into a narrow-necked 1 gallon (4½ litres) fermentation vessel. Discard solids. Top up to the neck with cold water. Fit cork or rubber bung and air lock filled with water, or sulphite solution (see page 39). Leave in the warm until fermentation is complete; this can take 4–5 weeks at an even temperature of 18°C (64°F).

Fermentation has finished when bubbles have ceased passing through the liquid in the air lock. A wine hydrometer reading (see page 44) of around 0.997 indicates fermentation may have ended. Check your red clover flower rosé tastes dry (non-sweet), is not fizzy on your tongue and is beginning to fall clear from the surface downwards.

When satisfied fermentation has finished, syphon or pour wine from its sediment into a narrow-necked one gallon (4½ litres) storage vessel. Top up to the neck with wine of a similar flavour and colour, or cold water. Fit a cork or rubber bung. Store somewhere cool to clear and mature before bottling.

Your red clover flower rosé should be clear and ready to bottle after about 6 months' storage, though a few months longer improves the wine's quality. When bottled, the wine needs a further 2–3 months to condition and mature before drinking.

Red clover flower rosé achieves peak excellence about 20 months after the fermented wine has been transferred to a storage vessel to clear and mature.

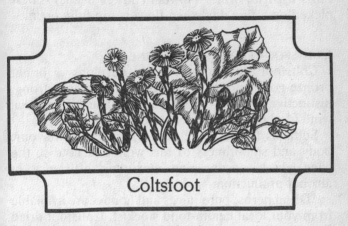

Coltsfoot

COLTSFOOT *(Tussilago farfara).*

Coltsfoot, named after the colt's foot shape of its leaves, has been credited with powerful medicinal properties since ancient times. Coltsfoot's generic name – Tussilago – derives from the Latin *tussis*, meaning a cough. Coltsfoot is a very pleasant natural country cure for coughs and colds.

Early American pioneer-settlers called coltsfoot "British tobacco". Dried coltsfoot leaves, gently packed in a smoker's pipe, give a long, cool and dry smoke – traditionally believed to help relieve asthma. Snuff made from powdered dried coltsfoot leaves was regarded as an especially effective way to clear sinuses and cure headache.

Coltsfoot is a perennial plant of around 6 inches (0.15m) in height. It likes most types of soil in a sunny or partly shaded position, and is widespread in the

wild. Coltsfoot's gold-yellow flowers precede the
plant's hoof-shaped leaves; the flowers bloom from
February to April.

Parts used for wine: Flowers (flower heads) – best
picked on a fine day when flowers are fully open.

COLTSFOOT FLOWER HERB WINE

Coltsfoot flower herb wine develops a bright
bronze-gold colour, with rich fragrance and strong,
distinctive flavour; enjoyable as an aperitif or social
wine of about 11.5% alcohol by volume.

Sultanas (dried white grapes) give extra flavour,
body and smoothness to this wine and nourish the
wine yeast, encouraging maximum efficiency in
alcohol production.

*Dried herbs, pure juices and honeys are available
from your local health-food stockist. Coltsfoot dried
flower heads are also available from home-brew
stockists.

INGREDIENTS: to make 1 gallon (4½ litres).
Fresh coltsfoot flower heads – 1 pint (½ litre)
  or *dried heads – 1 oz (28g)
Water – up to 1 gallon (4½ litres)
Granulated sugar *(optional, see below)* **– 1½ lb (680g)**
Tea, strong – ½ cup
Sultanas – 12 oz (340g)
***Pure pineapple juice – 1¾ pints (1 litre)**
Wine yeast – amount recommended by manufacturer

SUGAR-FREE "SECRET" RECIPE (see page 23): To
make coltsfoot flower herb wine without adding sugar
(sucrose) replace the entire quantity of granulated
sugar with **1 lb (454g) of *pure lime blossom or mixed**

blossom honey; and either 2¾ pints (1½ litres) of *pure white grape juice, or ¾ pint (426ml) of wine making concentrated white grape juice.

METHOD

Sterilise (see page 38) and *rinse* wine making equipment and utensils before use. To measure fresh coltsfoot heads (if used), remove and discard pieces of stalk and gently press heads in measuring jug. Lightly rinse fresh heads in cold water. Put fresh or dried heads in plastic (food grade) bucket. Cover. Warm 1 pint (½ litre) of water in large saucepan. Stir in granulated sugar or pure honey. When dissolved, cover and leave to cool. Make tea, strain and allow to cool, or use strained cold tea from an earlier brew. Discard tea leaves or bag. Rinse sultanas in warm water. Chop or mince sultanas. Pour pure pineapple juice and white grape juice (if used), brewed tea, and dissolved sugar or honey into bucket. Add sultanas, wine yeast and cold water to raise the total quantity of liquid to about 7 pints (4 litres). Allow at least 2 inches (51mm) – 4 inches (102mm) at the top of your bucket for the fermentation's initial frothing. Cover. Keep bucket in a warm place for 9 days. Stir twice daily.

After nine days pour or scoop the fermenting wine from its sediment and strain into a narrow-necked 1 gallon (4½ litres) fermentation vessel. Discard solids. Top up to the neck with cold water. Fit cork or rubber bung and air lock filled with water, or sulphite solution (see page 39). Leave in the warm until fermentation is complete; this can take 4–5 weeks at an even temperature of 18°C (64°F).

Fermentation has finished when bubbles have ceased passing through the liquid in the air lock. A wine hydrometer reading (see page 44) of around 0.997 indicates fermentation may have ended. Check your coltsfoot flower herb wine tastes dry (non-sweet), is not fizzy on your tongue and is beginning to fall clear from the surface downwards.

When satisfied fermentation has finished, syphon or pour wine from its sediment into a narrow-necked 1 gallon (4½ litres) storage vessel. Top up to the neck with wine of a similar flavour and colour, or cold water. Fit a cork or rubber bung. Store somewhere cool to clear and mature before bottling.

Your coltsfoot flower herb wine should be clear and ready to bottle after about 6 months' storage, though a few months longer improves the wine's quality. When bottled, the wine needs a further 2–3 months to condition and mature before drinking.

Coltsfoot flower herb wine achieves peak excellence about 18 months after the fermented wine has been transferred to a storage vessel to clear and mature.

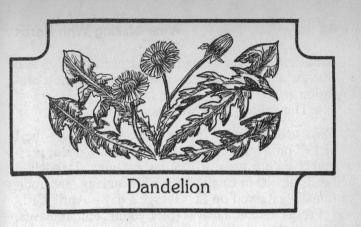

Dandelion

DANDELION *(Taraxacum officinale)*.

Dandelions are today dismissed by many people as bothersome "weeds". In ancient times the dandelion was highly esteemed for its considerable medicinal and culinary uses.

Every part of the dandelion has a beneficial application. The flowers flavour country wine, ale and salad; they also make excellent toilet waters and facial beauty lotions (to tone the skin). The roots and leaves brew a wonderful tonic ale, herbal tea; and add flavour and nutritional value to soup, stew and salad. Roasted roots are ground to make a delicious caffeine-free coffee-like drink. Milky sap from the flowering stem and leaves was once a popular remedy for eye troubles.

Commercial crops of dandelions are grown in France and the U.S.A.!

Dandelion is a perennial plant of around 10 inches (0.25m) in height. It likes nearly all types of soil and grows in almost any situation – common to meadows, pastures, waste land and gardens – particularly lawns! The dandelion's bright yellow flower head can bloom at any time of year, though March to October are

dandelions' favourite months – especially April and
May, when dandelion heads are seen in greatest pro-
fusion.
- Dandelions grow well indoors.

Parts used for wine: Flowers (flower heads) – best
picked on a bright day when flowers are open; preferably before noon if the day is sunny. Dandelion
heads picked in England for wine making, are traditionally gathered on St. George's day – April 23rd.

Fresh dandelion leaves (pick young, tender leaves;
best gathered from April–September) or dried
leaves, may be used in addition to flowers – bestowing
extra flavour, nutritional and medicinal value to dandelion flower rosé. Add ½ pint (284ml) of fresh
leaves, or ½ oz (14g) of dried leaves to the rosé
recipe. Any such addition is optional, and left to your
discretion.

DANDELION FLOWER ROSÉ
Dandelion flower rosé develops an attractive pale
red-gold colour, with delicate aroma and fresh flower-
grape flavour; enjoyable as an aperitif, table or social
wine of about 12.5% alcohol by volume.

Sultanas (dried white grapes) give extra flavour,
body and smoothness to this wine and nourish the
wine yeast, encouraging maximum efficiency in
alcohol production.

*Dried herbs, pure juices and honeys are available
from your local health-food stockist. Dandelion dried
flower heads are also available from home-brew
stockists.

INGREDIENTS: to make 1 gallon (4½ litres).
Fresh dandelion flower heads – 1¾ pints (1 litre)
  or *dried heads – 2 oz (56g)
Water – up to 1 gallon (4½ litres)
Granulated sugar *(optional, see below)* – 1½ lb (680g)
Tea, strong – ½ cup
Sultanas – 12 oz (340g)
Lemons – 2
*Pure red grape juice – 1¾ pints (1 litre)
Wine yeast – amount recommended by manufacturer

SUGAR-FREE "SECRET" RECIPE (see page 23): To
make dandelion flower rosé without adding sugar (sucrose) replace the entire quantity of granulated sugar
with **1 lb (454g) of *pure acacia blossom or mixed
blossom honey; and either 2¾ pints (1½ litres) of *pure
white grape juice, or ¾ pint (426ml) of wine making
concentrated white grape juice.**

METHOD
  Sterilise (see page 38) and *rinse* wine making equipment and utensils before use. To measure fresh dandelion heads (if used), remove and discard pieces of
green leaf and stalk and gently press heads in measuring jug. Lightly rinse fresh heads in cold water. Put
fresh or dried heads in plastic (food grade) bucket.
Cover. Warm 1 pint (½ litre) of water in large saucepan. Stir in granulated sugar or pure honey. When
dissolved, cover and leave to cool. Make tea, strain
and allow to cool, or use strained cold tea from an
earlier brew. Discard tea leaves or bag. Rinse sultanas
in warm water. Chop or mince sultanas. Extract juice
from lemons. Discard pips, pith and peel. Pour pure
red grape juice and white grape juice (if used), lemon
juice, brewed tea, and dissolved sugar or honey into

bucket. Add sultanas, wine yeast and cold water to raise the total quantity of liquid to about 7 pints (4 litres). Allow at least 2 inches (51mm) – 4 inches (102mm) at the top of your bucket for the fermentation's initial frothing. Cover. Keep bucket in a warm place for 9 days. Stir twice daily.

After nine days pour or scoop the fermenting wine from its sediment and strain into a narrow-necked 1 gallon (4½ litres) fermentation vessel. Discard solids. Top up to the neck with cold water. Fit cork or rubber bung and air lock filled with water, or sulphite solution (see page 39). Leave in the warm until fermentation is complete; this can take 4–5 weeks at an even temperature of 18°C (64°F).

Fermentation has finished when bubbles have ceased passing through the liquid in the air lock. A wine hydrometer reading (see page 44) of around 0.997 indicates fermentation may have ended. Check your dandelion flower rosé tastes dry (non-sweet), is not fizzy on your tongue and is beginning to fall clear from the surface downwards.

When satisfied fermentation has finished, syphon or pour wine from its sediment into a narrow-necked one gallon (4½ litres) storage vessel. Top up to the neck with wine of a similar flavour and colour, or cold water. Fit a cork or rubber bung. Store somewhere cool to clear and mature before bottling.

Your dandelion flower rosé should be clear and ready to bottle after about 6 months' storage, though a few months longer improves the wine's quality. When bottled, the wine needs a further 2–3 months to condition and mature before drinking.

Dandelion flower rosé achieves peak excellence about 20 months after the fermented wine has been transferred to a storage vessel to clear and mature.

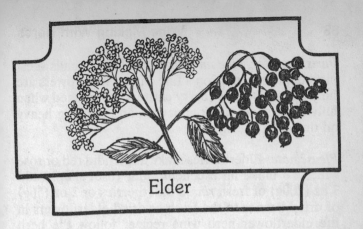

Elder

ELDER *(Sambucus nigra)*.

The elder is an important ancient holy tree, sacred to The Lady or "Earth Mother", the supreme female deity of Britain's pre-Christian pagan religions. Witches' magic wands (for general spell casting) are traditionally cut from the elder.

Every part of the elder has medicinal, culinary or practical value: wood, bark, leaves, flowers, berries and roots.

The delicately perfumed elderflowers make delicious country wine, cider, and ale; and add flavour to non-alcoholic beverages, green or fruit salad, stewed fruit, and sandwiches. Elderberries (used by the Romans to dye hair) enhance the flavour and nutritional value of fruit pies, puddings, jam, jelly and medium quality commercial red wines, particularly "cheap" port.

Elders are perennial, deciduous (shed leaves annually) shrubs or small trees of 6½–30 feet (2–9 metres) in height. The elder likes moist soil in a sunny position; it grows in hedgerows, grows wild in woodland and waste places, and merits a nook in gardens. The elder's cream-white flowers bloom in June and July. Elderberries ripen from September to October.

Parts used for wine and liqueur: Flower heads (best picked mid-morning on a fine day – when flowers are fully open). Berries (berry clusters best picked when fully ripe: shiny black, juicy-fat and hanging heavy on drooping stalks).

Please note: Elderberries make a splendid red or rosé wine. To make an excellent elder rosé, simply add 7 oz (200g) of fresh *rinsed* elderberries or 2 oz (56g) of dried berries to the fresh or dried elderflowers in the elderflower herb wine recipe, follow the herb wine instructions. Any such addition is optional, and left to your discretion.

To harvest fresh elderberries use strong scissors to cut stalks supporting berry clusters. Take care as elderberry juice stains! At home wear an apron and rubber or plastic gloves to handle fresh elderberries (and dried elderberries after soaking in water). Strip fresh elderberries from stalks with a table fork.

Rinse *dried* elderberries (if used) in warm water; then soak the dried berries in cold water for 24 hours before use. Dried elderberries are available from health-food and home-brew stockists.

ELDERFLOWER HERB WINE

Elderflower herb wine develops an alluring pale gold-yellow colour, with honey-sweet fragrance and enchanting fresh flavour; enjoyable as an aperitif, table or social wine of about 11.5% alcohol by volume.

Sultanas (dried white grapes) give extra flavour, body and smoothness to this wine and nourish the wine yeast, encouraging maximum efficiency in alcohol production.

*Dried herbs, pure juices and honeys are available from your local health food stockist. Dried elderflowers are also available from home-brew stockists.

INGREDIENTS: to make 1 gallon (4½ litres).
Fresh elderflower heads – ¾ pint (426ml)
   or *dried elderflowers – ¾ oz (21g)
Water – up to 1 gallon (4½ litres)
Granulated sugar *(optional, see below)* **– 1½ lb (680g)**
Tea, strong – ½ cup
Sultanas – 12 oz (340g)
Lemons – 2
***Pure apple juice – 1¾ pints (1 litre)**
Wine yeast – amount recommended by manufacturer

SUGAR-FREE "SECRET" RECIPE (see page 23): To make elderflower herb wine without adding sugar (sucrose) replace the entire quantity of granulated sugar with **1 lb (454g) of *pure acacia blossom or lime blossom honey; and either 2¾ pints (1½ litres) of *pure white grape juice, or ¾ pint (426ml) of wine making concentrated white grape juice.**

METHOD
Sterilise (see page 38) and *rinse* wine making equipment and utensils before use. To measure fresh elderflower heads (if used), remove and discard pieces of stalk and gently press heads in measuring jug. Lightly rinse fresh heads in cold water. Put fresh or dried heads in plastic (food grade) bucket. Cover. Warm 1 pint (½ litre) of water in large saucepan. Stir in granulated sugar or pure honey. When dissolved, cover and leave to cool. Make tea, strain and allow to cool, or use strained cold tea from an earlier brew. Discard tea leaves or bag. Rinse sultanas in warm

water. Chop or mince sultanas. Extract juice from
lemons. Discard pips, pith and peel. Pour pure apple
juice and white grape juice (if used), lemon juice,
brewed tea, and dissolved sugar or honey into bucket.
Add sultanas, wine yeast and cold water to raise the
total quantity of liquid to about 7 pints (4 litres).
Allow at least 2 inches (51mm) – 4 inches (102mm)
at the top of your bucket for the fermentation's initial
frothing. Cover. Keep bucket in a warm place for 9
days. Stir twice daily.

After nine days pour or scoop the fermenting wine
from its sediment and strain into a narrow-necked
1 gallon (4½ litres) fermentation vessel. Discard solids.
Top up to the neck with cold water. Fit cork or rubber
bung and air lock filled with water, or sulphite solution (see page 39). Leave in the warm until fermentation is complete; this can take 4–5 weeks at an even
temperature of 18°C (64°F).

Fermentation has finished when bubbles have
ceased passing through the liquid in the air lock. A
wine hydrometer reading (see page 44) of around
0.997 indicates fermentation may have ended. Check
your elderflower herb wine tastes dry (non-sweet),
is not fizzy on your tongue and is beginning to fall
clear from the surface downwards.

When satisfied fermentation has finished, syphon
or pour wine from its sediment into a narrow-necked
1 gallon (4½ litres) storage vessel. Top up to the neck
with wine of a similar flavour and colour, or cold
water. Fit a cork or rubber bung. Store somewhere
cool to clear and mature before bottling.

Your elderflower herb wine should be clear and
ready to bottle after about 6 months' storage, though
a few months longer improves the wine's quality.
When bottled, the wine needs a further 2–3 months

to condition and mature before drinking.

Elderflower herb wine achieves peak excellence about 18 months after the fermented wine has been transferred to a storage vessel to clear and mature.

ELDER LIQUEUR

Elder liqueur is a fiery red colour, with exquisite fragrance and rich, heart-warming taste. Alcoholic strength (when brandy of around 40% Vol is used) about 23% alcohol by volume. Stronger brandy produces a more potent liqueur!

*Dried elderflowers, elderberries, liquorice root, spices, pure juice and honeys are available from your local health-food stockist. Dried elderflowers and elderberries are also available from home-brew stockists.

INGREDIENTS: to make 1 standard-size wine bottle.
*Dried elderberries – 1 oz (28g)
   or fresh berries – 3 oz (85g)
Fresh elderflower heads – 1 heaped tablespoon
   or *dried elderflowers – 1 level 5ml teaspoon
*Pure red grape juice – 6 fl oz (170ml)
*Pure mixed blossom or clover honey – 4 heaped
   tablespoons
Cinnamon (ground) – ¼ level 5ml teaspoon
Ginger (ground) – ¼ level 5ml teaspoon
Nutmeg (ground) – ¼ level 5ml teaspoon
Pure lemon juice – 2 level 5ml teaspoons
*Liquorice root, whole (dried) – 2 of average size –
   about 5″ (127mm) long and ¼″ (6mm) thick
Clove (whole) – 1
Brandy – 17 fl oz (483ml)

**Large jar (with tight-fitting lid) – big enough to hold
all ingredients, or one empty 1 litre wine, spirit or
cider bottle (in which to macerate ingredients) and
cork or plastic stopper.**

METHOD

Sterilise (see page 38) and *rinse* utensils before use.
Rinse dried elderberries (if used) in warm water; then
soak dried berries in cold water for 24 hours before
use. Lightly rinse fresh berries (if used – see fresh
elderberry harvesting and stripping note on page 88)
or fresh elderflowers in cold water. Warm grape juice
in small saucepan. Stir in honey, cinnamon, ginger,
nutmeg and lemon juice. When dissolved, cover and
allow to cool. Rinse liquorice root in warm water,
then break into ½ inch (13mm) pieces and crush with
rolling pin or hammer. Place elderflowers, berries,
liquorice, clove, then brandy and lastly juice-honey
mixture in jar or bottle (use a plastic funnel for
liquid). Fasten lid or stopper. Store somewhere warm
for 10 days. Then strain liqueur through a fine-mesh
strainer into a large jug. Squeeze liquid from flowers,
berries and soft liquorice root. Discard solids. Pour
the cloudy liqueur through a plastic funnel into an
empty wine bottle. Stopper the bottle with a cork or
plastic stopper. Store in a cool place for 13 weeks to
clear and permit the flavours to blend and mellow.
Then syphon or carefully pour the liqueur from its
sediment into a large jug; filter (see page 50) liqueur
through a plastic funnel into an empty wine or liqueur
bottle – fasten a cork or plastic stopper.

Your Elder Liqueur is now ready to enjoy, and
should continue to improve in quality for a further
9–12 weeks, before achieving peak excellence. Serve
at room temperature in liqueur glasses. Good health!

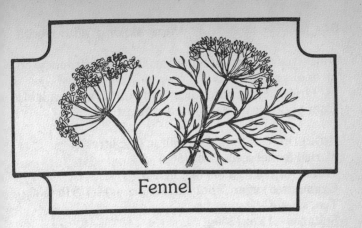

Fennel

FENNEL *Foeniculum vulgare)*.

Oil from fennel seeds is used to flavour commercial liqueurs (including Absinthe and Anisette), and it is used in perfumes, beauty soaps, lotions and scents. Fennel seeds flavour foods such as bread, cakes, pastry, fish, sweet pickle, stews, sauces, soups and sweets.

Fennel is a perennial plant of around 3 feet (1 metre) in height. It likes rich, well-drained soil in a sunny position. Fennel's yellow flowers bloom from July to September.

● Fennel grows well indoors.

Parts used for wine and liqueur: Seeds; harvest when ripe – July onwards. Dry fresh seeds in a warm place, see page 30 – before use.

FENNEL SEED HERB WINE

Fennel seed herb wine develops a rich yellow-gold colour, with fruity aroma and exotic, liquorice-like flavour; enjoyable as an aperitif or social wine of about 11.5% alcohol by volume.

Sultanas (dried white grapes) give extra flavour, body and smoothness to this wine and nourish the wine yeast, encouraging maximum efficiency in alcohol production.

*Dried herbs, pure juices and honeys are available from your local health-food stockist.

INGREDIENTS: to make 1 gallon (4½ litres).
Dried fennel seed – 2 oz (56g)
Water – up to 1 gallon (4½ litres)
Granulated sugar *(optional, see below)* **– 1½ lb (680g)**
Tea, strong – ½ cup
Sultanas – 12 oz (340g)
*Pure pineapple juice – 1¾ pints (1 litre)
Wine yeast – amount recommended by manufacturer

SUGAR-FREE "SECRET" RECIPE (see page 23): To make fennel seed herb wine without adding sugar (sucrose) replace the entire quantity of granulated sugar with **1 lb (454g) of *pure lime blossom or acacia blossom honey; and either 2¾ pints (1½ litres) of *pure white grape juice, or ¾ pint (426ml) of wine making concentrated white grape juice.**

METHOD
Sterilise (see page 38) and *rinse* wine making equipment and utensils before use. Place fennel seeds in plastic (food grade) bucket. Cover. Warm 1 pint (½ litre) of water in large saucepan. Stir in granulated sugar or pure honey. When dissolved, cover and leave to cool. Make tea, strain and allow to cool, or use strained cold tea from an earlier brew. Discard tea leaves or bag. Rinse sultanas in warm water. Chop or mince sultanas. Pour pure pineapple juice, and grape juice (if used), brewed tea, and dissolved sugar or honey into bucket. Add sultanas, wine yeast and cold water to raise the total quantity of liquid to about

7 pints (4 litres). Allow at least 2 inches (51mm) – 4 inches (102mm) at the top of your bucket for the fermentation's initial frothing. Cover. Keep bucket in a warm place for 10 days. Stir twice daily.

After ten days pour or scoop the fermenting wine from its sediment and strain into a narrow-necked 1 gallon (4½ litres) fermentation vessel. Discard solids. Top up to the neck with cold water. Fit cork or rubber bung and air lock filled with water, or sulphite solution (see page 39). Leave in the warm until fermentation is complete; this can take 4–5 weeks at an even temperature of 18°C (64°F).

Fermentation has finished when bubbles have ceased passing through the liquid in the air lock. A wine hydrometer reading (see page 44) of around 0.997 indicates fermentation may have ended. Check your fennel seed herb wine tastes dry (non-sweet), is not fizzy on your tongue and is beginning to fall clear from the surface downwards.

When satisfied fermentation has finished, syphon or pour wine from its sediment into a narrow-necked one gallon (4½ litres) storage vessel. Top up to the neck with wine of a similar flavour and colour, or cold water. Fit a cork or rubber bung. Store somewhere cool to clear and mature before bottling.

Your fennel seed herb wine should be clear and ready to bottle after about 5 months' storage, though a few months longer improves the wine's quality. When bottled, the wine needs a further 2–3 months to condition and mature before drinking.

Fennel seed herb wine achieves peak excellence about 18 months after the fermented wine has been transferred to a storage vessel to clear and mature.

FENNEL DARK-RUM LIQUEUR

Fennel dark-rum liqueur has an exotic, spicy aroma; glows red in the glass and excites the senses with the warmth of its explosive Caribbean-fire-cracker flavour. Alcoholic strength (when dark-rum of around 40% Vol is used) about 23% alcohol by volume. Stronger dark-rum produces a more potent liqueur!

*Dried fennel seeds, spices, pure juice and honeys are available from your local health-food stockist.

INGREDIENTS: to make 1 standard-size wine bottle.
*Pure red grape juice – 6 fl oz (170ml)
*Pure orange blossom or mixed blossom honey –
   4 heaped tablespoons
Cinnamon (ground) – ¼ level 5ml teaspoon
Coriander (ground) – ¼ level 5ml teaspoon
Nutmeg (ground) – ¼ level 5ml teaspoon
Pure lemon juice – 2 level 5ml teaspoons
*Dried fennel seed – 1 oz (28g)
Dark-Rum – 17 fl oz (483ml)

Large jar (with tight-fitting lid) – big enough to hold all ingredients, or one empty 1 litre wine, spirit or cider bottle (in which to macerate ingredients) and cork or plastic stopper.

METHOD

Sterilise (see page 38) and *rinse* utensils before use. Warm grape juice in small saucepan. Stir in honey, cinnamon, coriander, nutmeg and lemon juice. When dissolved, cover and allow to cool. Place fennel seeds, then dark-rum and lastly juice-honey mixture in jar or bottle (use a plastic funnel for liquid). Fasten lid or stopper. Store somewhere warm for 10 days. Then strain liqueur through a fine-mesh strainer into a large jug. Discard solids. Pour the cloudy liqueur through a plastic funnel into an empty wine bottle. Stopper the bottle with a cork or plastic stopper. Store in a cool place for 9 weeks to clear and permit the flavours to blend and mellow. Then syphon or carefully pour the liqueur from its sediment into a large jug; filter (see page 50) liqueur through a plastic funnel into an empty wine or liqueur bottle – fasten a cork or plastic stopper.

Your Fennel Dark-Rum Liqueur is now ready to enjoy, and should continue to improve in quality for a further 9–12 weeks, before achieving peak excellence. Serve at room temperature in liqueur glasses. Good health!

Golden-rod

GOLDEN-ROD (*Solidago virgaurea* and *Solidago odora*).

Golden-rod makes a traditional, noble country wine and refreshing herbal tea.

Golden-rod is a perennial plant that can reach

2 feet (0.60) in height. It likes dry soil in a sunny position and grows wild in woodlands, on heaths; around hedges and rocks. Golden-rod's gold-yellow flowers bloom from July to September.

Parts used for wine: Leaves (gather from June to September – young leaves are best). Golden-rod flowers may be used in addition to leaves, bestowing extra aroma and flavour to golden-rod wine – add ½ pint (284ml) of fresh flower heads, or ½ oz (14g) of dried heads to the herb wine recipe. Any such addition is optional, and left to your discretion.

GOLDEN-ROD HERB WINE

Golden-rod herb (leaf) wine develops a fire-red colour, with pleasant aroma and strong, biting taste; enjoyable as an aperitif or social wine of about 12.5% alcohol by volume.

Raisins (dried black grapes) give extra flavour, body and smoothness to this wine and nourish the wine yeast, encouraging maximum efficiency in alcohol production.

*Dried herbs, pure juices and honeys are available from your local health-food stockist.

INGREDIENTS: to make 1 gallon (4½ litres).
Fresh golden-rod leaves – ½ pint (284ml)
    or *dried leaves – ½ oz (14g)
Water – up to 1 gallon (4½ litres)
Granulated sugar *(optional, see below)* **– 1½ lb (680g)**
Tea, strong – ½ cup
Raisins – 12 oz (340g)
Lemons – 2
***Pure red grape juice – 1¾ pints (1 litre)**
Wine yeast – amount recommended by manufacturer

SUGAR-FREE "SECRET" RECIPE (see page 23): To make golden-rod herb wine without adding sugar (sucrose) replace the entire quantity of granulated sugar with **1 lb (454g) of *pure clover or mixed blossom honey; and either 2¾ pints (1½ litres) of *pure red grape juice, or ¾ pint (426ml) of wine making concentrated red grape juice.**

METHOD

Sterilise (see page 38) and *rinse* wine making equipment and utensils before use. To measure fresh golden-rod leaves (if used), gently press leaves in measuring jug. Lightly rinse fresh leaves in cold water. Put fresh or dried leaves in plastic (food grade) bucket. Cover. Warm 1 pint (½ litre) of water in large saucepan. Stir in granulated sugar or pure honey. When dissolved, cover and leave to cool. Make tea, strain and allow to cool, or use strained cold tea from an earlier brew. Discard tea leaves or bag. Rinse raisins in warm water. Chop or mince raisins. Extract juice from lemons. Discard pips, pith and peel. Pour red grape juice, lemon juice, brewed tea, and dissolved sugar or honey into bucket. Add raisins, wine yeast and cold water to raise the total quantity of liquid to about 7 pints (4 litres). Allow at least 2 inches (51mm) – 4 inches (102mm) at the top of your bucket for the fermentation's initial frothing. Cover. Keep bucket in a warm place for 7 days. Stir twice daily.

After seven days pour or scoop the fermenting wine from its sediment and strain into a narrow-necked 1 gallon (4½ litres) fermentation vessel. Discard solids. Top up to the neck with cold water. Fit cork or rubber bung and air lock filled with water, or sulphite solution (see page 39). Leave in the warm until fermen-

tation is complete; this can take 4–5 weeks at an even temperature of 18°C (64°F).

Fermentation has finished when bubbles have ceased passing through the liquid in the air lock. A wine hydrometer reading (see page 44) of around 0.997 indicates fermentation may have ended. Check your golden-rod herb wine tastes dry (non-sweet), is not fizzy on your tongue and is beginning to fall clear from the surface downwards.

When satisfied fermentation has finished, syphon or pour wine from its sediment into a narrow-necked one gallon (4½ litres) storage vessel. Top up to the neck with wine of a similar flavour and colour, or cold water. Fit a cork or rubber bung. Store somewhere cool to clear and mature before bottling.

Your golden-rod herb wine should be clear and ready to bottle after about 7 months' storage, though a few months longer improves the wine's quality. When bottled, the wine needs a further 2–3 months to condition and mature before drinking.

Golden-rod herb wine achieves peak excellence about 22 months after the fermented wine has been transferred to a storage vessel to clear and mature.

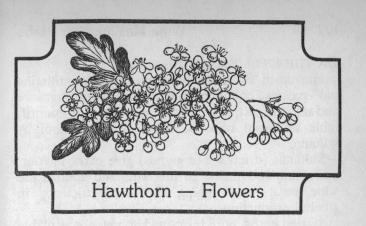

Hawthorn — Flowers

HAWTHORN *(Crataegus monogyna)*.

Hawthorns have been revered as holy shrubs or trees, blessed with special protective and healing properties, since ancient times. Greeks of pre-Christian civilisation gave sprigs of hawthorn blossom as a token of happiness and prosperity. Moses heard God speak from a "burning" hawthorn *(Crataegus pyracantha)*. Jesus of Nazareth's crown of thorns was cut from a hawthorn. The Pilgrim Fathers (102 colonists), founders of modern America, sailed from Southampton, England (1620) in a boat named "Mayflower". Mayflower or mayblossom is a common name for the hawthorn's flowers.

Hawthorns are hardy, perennial shrubs or small trees; popularly planted as hedges. They are also found in woodland and fields. Hawthorns like well-drained soil in a sunny position. The hawthorn's strong-scented white or pink flowers blossom in May and June. The dark-red berries or "haws" ripen in autumn.

Parts used for wine and liqueur: Flowers (best picked mid-morning on a dry day) and berries (gather when ripe – September to October).

HAWTHORN BLOSSOM ROSÉ

Hawthorn blossom rosé develops a scintillating pale-red rosé colour, with a sweet-scented fragrance and smooth, distinctive taste; enjoyable as an aperitif, table or social wine of about 12.5% alcohol by volume.

Sultanas (dried white grapes) give extra flavour, body and smoothness to this wine and nourish the wine yeast, encouraging maximum efficiency in alcohol production.

*Dried herbs, pure juices and honeys are available from your local health-food stockist.

INGREDIENTS: to make 1 gallon (4½ litres).
Fresh hawthorn flowers – 1¾ pints (1 litre)
    or *dried flowers – 2 oz (56g)
Water – up to 1 gallon (4½ litres)
Granulated sugar (*optional, see below*) **– 1½ lb (680g)**
Tea, strong – ½ cup
Sultanas – 12 oz (340g)
Lemons – 2
***Pure red grape juice – 1¾ pints (1 litre)**
Wine yeast – amount recommended by manufacturer

SUGAR-FREE "SECRET" RECIPE (see page 23): To make hawthorn blossom rosé without adding sugar (sucrose) replace the entire quantity of granulated sugar with **1 lb (454g) of *pure acacia blossom or lime blossom honey; and either 2¾ pints (1½ litres) of *pure white grape juice, or ¾ pint (426ml) of wine making concentrated white grape juice.**

METHOD

Sterilise (see page 38) and *rinse* wine making equipment and utensils before use. To measure fresh hawthorn flowers (if used), discard pieces of green leaf and stalk and gently press flowers in measuring jug. Lightly rinse fresh flowers in cold water. Put fresh or dried flowers in plastic (food grade) bucket. Cover. Warm 1 pint (½ litre) of water in large saucepan. Stir in granulated sugar or pure honey. When dissolved, cover and leave to cool. Make tea, strain and allow to cool, or use strained cold tea from an earlier brew. Discard tea leaves or bag. Rinse sultanas in warm water. Chop or mince sultanas. Extract juice from lemons. Discard pips, pith and peel. Pour pure red grape juice and white grape juice (if used), lemon juice, brewed tea, and dissolved sugar or honey into bucket. Add sultanas, wine yeast and cold water to raise the total quantity of liquid to about 7 pints (4 litres). Allow at least 2 inches (51mm) – 4 inches (102mm) at the top of your bucket for the fermentation's initial frothing. Cover. Keep bucket in a warm place for 9 days. Stir twice daily.

After nine days pour or scoop the fermenting wine from its sediment and strain into a narrow-necked 1 gallon (4½ litres) fermentation vessel. Discard solids. Top up to the neck with cold water. Fit cork or rubber bung and air lock filled with water, or sulphite solution (see page 39). Leave in the warm until fermentation is complete; this can take 4–5 weeks at an even temperature of 18°C (64°F).

Fermentation has finished when bubbles have ceased passing through the liquid in the air lock. A wine hydrometer reading (see page 44) of around 0.997 indicates fermentation may have ended. Check your hawthorn blossom rosé tastes dry (non-sweet), is not fizzy on your tongue and is beginning to fall clear from the surface downwards.

When satisfied fermentation has finished, syphon or pour wine from its sediment into a narrow-necked one gallon (4½ litres) storage vessel. Top up to the neck with wine of a similar flavour and colour, or cold water. Fit a cork or rubber bung. Store somewhere cool to clear and mature before bottling.

Your hawthorn blossom rosé should be clear and ready to bottle after about 5 months' storage, though a few months longer improves the wine's quality. When bottled, the wine needs a further 2–3 months to condition and mature before drinking.

Hawthorn blossom rosé achieves peak excellence about 18 months after the fermented wine has been transferred to a storage vessel to clear and mature.

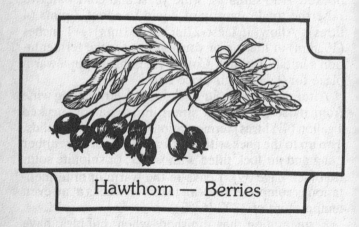

Hawthorn — Berries

THE MAYFLOWER LIQUEUR

The Mayflower liqueur is a deep-bronze colour, with entrancing fragrance and warm fruit-spice taste. Alcoholic strength (when brandy of around 40% Vol is used) about 23% alcohol by volume. Stronger brandy produces a more potent liqueur!

*Dried hawthorn flowers (blossom), berries ("haws"), spices, pure juice and honeys are available from your local health-food stockist.

INGREDIENTS: to make 1 standard-size wine bottle.
*Dried hawthorn berries ("haws") – 1 oz (28g)
   or fresh berries – 2 oz (56g)
Fresh hawthorn flowers – ½ pint (284ml)
   or *dried flowers (blossom) – ½ oz (14g)
*Pure pineapple juice – 6 fl oz (170ml)
*Pure acacia blossom or mixed blossom honey –
   4 heaped tablespoons
Cinnamon (ground) – ½ level 5ml teaspoon
Cloves (whole) – 2
Brandy – 17 fl oz (483ml)

Large jar (with tight-fitting lid) – big enough to hold all ingredients, or one empty 1 litre wine, spirit or cider bottle (in which to macerate ingredients) and cork or plastic stopper.

METHOD
   Sterilise (see page 38) and *rinse* utensils before use. Rinse dried hawthorn berries (if used) in warm water; then soak dried berries in cold water for 24 hours before use. To measure fresh hawthorn flowers (if used), remove and discard pieces of green leaf and stalk and gently press fresh flowers in measuring jug. Remove and discard pieces of stalk from fresh berries (if used). Lightly rinse fresh hawthorn flowers or fresh berries in cold water. Warm pineapple juice in small saucepan. Stir in honey and cinnamon. When dissolved, cover and allow to cool. Prick fresh or dried

(soaked and softened) hawthorn berries several times with a sharp sewing-needle (or similar instrument). Place hawthorn flowers, berries, cloves, then brandy and lastly juice-honey mixture in jar or bottle (use a plastic funnel for liquid). Fasten lid or stopper. Store somewhere warm for 10 days. Then strain liqueur through a fine-mesh strainer into a large jug. Squeeze liquid from flowers and berries. Discard solids. Pour the cloudy liqueur through a plastic funnel into an empty wine bottle. Stopper the bottle with a cork or plastic stopper. Store in a cool place for 9 weeks to clear and permit the flavours to blend and mellow. Then syphon or carefully pour the liqueur from its sediment into a large jug; filter (see page 50) liqueur through a plastic funnel into an empty wine or liqueur bottle – fasten a cork or plastic stopper.

The Mayflower Liqueur is now ready to enjoy, and should continue to improve in quality for a further 9–12 weeks, before achieving peak excellence. Serve at room temperature in liqueur glasses. Good sailing!

Hop

HOP *(Humulus lupulus)*.

Hops are commercially cultivated to flavour beer. Hops can be used to flavour salad, broth, stew and bread. A "herb pillow" stuffed with dried hops, is a traditional remedy for insomnia and earache.

The hop vine is a perennial climber, which can reach 16½ feet (5 metres) in height. It likes rich, well-watered soil in a sunny position. Wild hops grow in hedges, thickets and at the edge of woodland and forest – in damp places.

Male and female flowers grow on separate plants. The green-yellow-brown flower-cones of the female plant are called hops; the hop cones appear from July to August.

Parts used for wine: Female flowers (hop cones – *hops*). Hops are best picked in August. Remove and discard pieces of stalk; dry fresh hops in a warm place (see page 29) before use – to reduce the strong flavour of fresh-picked hops. 10 oz (283g) of fresh hops dry to about 2 oz (56g).

HOP HERB WINE

Hop herb wine develops a delightful green-gold colour, with appetising fruit-hop aroma and soothing

107

taste; enjoyable as an aperitif or social wine of about
11.5% alcohol by volume.

Sultanas (dried white grapes) give extra flavour,
body and smoothness to this wine and nourish the
wine yeast, encouraging maximum efficiency in
alcohol production.

*Dried herbs, pure juices and honeys are available
from your local health-food stockist. Dried hops are
also available from home-brew stockists.

INGREDIENTS: to make 1 gallon (4½ litres).
Dried hops – 2 oz (56g)
Water – up to 1 gallon (4½ litres)
Granulated sugar (optional, see below) **– 1½ lb (680g)**
Tea, strong – ½ cup
Sultanas – 12 oz (340g)
***Pure pineapple juice – 1¾ pints (1 litre)**
Wine yeast – amount recommended by manufacturer

SUGAR-FREE "SECRET" RECIPE (see page 23): To
make hop herb wine without adding sugar (sucrose)
replace the entire quantity of granulated sugar with
**1 lb (454g) of *pure lime blossom or acacia blossom
honey; and either 2¾ pints (1½ litres) of *pure white
grape juice, or ¾ pint (426ml) of wine making concentrated white grape juice.**

METHOD

Sterilise (see page 38) and *rinse* wine making equipment and utensils before use. Put dried hops in plastic
(food grade) bucket. Cover. Warm 1 pint (½ litre)
of water in large saucepan. Stir in granulated sugar
or pure honey. When dissolved, cover and leave to
cool. Make tea, strain and allow to cool, or use
strained cold tea from an earlier brew. Discard tea

leaves or bag. Rinse sultanas in warm water. Chop or mince sultanas. Pour pure pineapple juice, and grape juice (if used), brewed tea, and dissolved sugar or honey into bucket. Add sultanas, wine yeast and cold water to raise the total quantity of liquid to about 7 pints (4 litres). Allow at least 2 inches (51mm) – 4 inches (102mm) at the top of your bucket for the fermentation's initial frothing. Cover. Keep bucket in a warm place for 7 days. Stir twice daily.

After seven days pour or scoop the fermenting wine from its sediment and strain into a narrow-necked 1 gallon (4½ litres) fermentation vessel. Discard solids. Top up to the neck with cold water. Fit cork or rubber bung and air lock filled with water, or sulphite solution (see page 39). Leave in the warm until fermentation is complete; this can take 4–5 weeks at an even temperature of 18°C (64°F).

Fermentation has finished when bubbles have ceased passing through the liquid in the air lock. A wine hydrometer reading (see page 44) of around 0.997 indicates fermentation may have ended. Check your hop herb wine tastes dry (non-sweet), is not fizzy on your tongue and is beginning to fall clear from the surface downwards.

When satisfied fermentation has finished, syphon or pour wine from its sediment into a narrow-necked 1 gallon (4½ litres) storage vessel. Top up to the neck with wine of a similar flavour and colour, or cold water. Fit a cork or rubber bung. Store somewhere cool to clear and mature before bottling.

Your hop herb wine should be clear and ready to bottle after about 6 months' storage, though a few months longer improves the wine's quality. When bottled, the wine needs a further 2–3 months to condition and mature before drinking.

Hop herb wine achieves peak excellence about 20 months after the fermented wine has been transferred to a storage vessel to clear and mature.

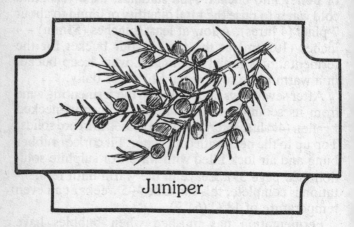

Juniper

JUNIPER *(Juniperus communis)*.

Juniper berries flavour commercial liqueurs; meat, game and fish dishes; and sauces and stuffings.

Juniper berries are the principal ingredient in gin. The English word "gin" derives from the Dutch "genever" and French genièvre (Juniper). Gin was created by Professor Franciscus Sylvius (1614–72) of the University of Lyden, Holland. Professor Sylvius intended gin to be a cheap medicine – a powerful diuretic! Gin (the diuretic medicine) became popular with seventeenth century English troops stationed in The Netherlands hence another alcoholic beverage was born!

Juniper berries are fruits of the Juniper perennial evergreen shrub or small tree, which usually reaches 6½–10 feet (2–3 metres) in height, though it can grow taller. Juniper male shrubs produce small yellow flowers from May to June; female shrubs produce green flowers.

Juniper berries follow the green flowers on female shrubs; beginning life as green berry-like cones, and not maturing into blue-black berries until their second year.

Parts used for liqueur: Blue-black berries (pick when fully ripe – October to November).

LIQUEUR DE GENIÈVRE

Juniper liqueur is an inviting yellow-gold colour, with delicate aroma and exciting biting spice-fruit tang. Alcoholic strength (when brandy of around 40% Vol is used) about 23% alcohol by volume. Stronger brandy produces a more potent liqueur!

*Dried juniper berries, spices, pure juice and honeys are available from your local health-food stockist. Dried juniper berries are also available from home-brew stockists.

INGREDIENTS: to make 1 standard-size wine bottle.
*Dried juniper berries – 2 oz (57g)
   or fresh berries – 4 oz (113g)
*Pure apple juice – 6 fl oz (170ml)
*Pure acacia blossom or mixed blossom honey –
   4 heaped tablespoons
Ginger (ground) – ¼ level 5ml teaspoon
Nutmeg (ground) – ½ level 5ml teaspoon
Pure lemon juice – 2 level 5ml teaspoons
Brandy – 17 fl oz (483ml)

Large jar (with tight-fitting lid) – big enough to hold all ingredients, or one empty 1 litre wine, spirit or cider bottle (in which to macerate ingredients) and cork or plastic stopper.

METHOD

Sterilise (see page 38) and *rinse* utensils before use. Rinse dried juniper berries (if used) in warm water; then soak dried berries in cold water for 24 hours before use. Remove and discard fresh juniper berry stalks. Lightly rinse fresh berries in cold water. Warm apple juice in small saucepan. Stir in honey, ginger, nutmeg and lemon juice. When dissolved, cover and allow to cool. Prick fresh or dried (soaked and softened) juniper berries several times with a sharp sewing-needle (or similar instrument). Place juniper berries, then brandy and lastly juice-honey mixture in jar or bottle (use a plastic funnel for liquid). Fasten lid or stopper. Store somewhere warm for 10 days. Then strain liqueur through a fine-mesh strainer into a large jug. Squeeze liquid from berries. Discard solids. Pour the cloudy liqueur through a plastic funnel into an empty wine bottle. Stopper the bottle with a cork or plastic stopper. Store in a cool place for 9 weeks to clear and permit the flavours to blend and mellow. Then syphon or carefully pour the liqueur from its sediment into a large jug; filter (see page 50) liqueur through a plastic funnel into an empty wine or liqueur bottle – fasten a cork or plastic stopper.

Your Liqueur De Genièvre is now ready to enjoy, and should continue to improve in quality for a further 9–12 weeks, before achieving peak excellence. Serve at room temperature in liqueur glasses. Cheers!

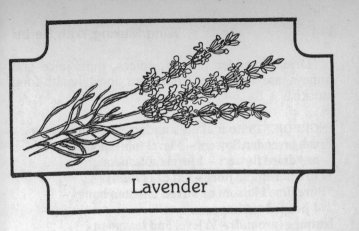

Lavender

LAVENDER *(Lavandula officinalis)*.

Ancient Greeks and Romans bathed and scented their bodies with sweet-smelling lavender water. Oil from lavender flowers is used in many of today's commercial perfumes and cosmetics. Lavender flowers and leaves flavour popular Southern European dishes and contribute to the beautiful fragrance of pot-pourris, bath salts and toilet waters.

Lavender is a perennial small shrub of around 2½ feet (0.75m) in height. It likes dry, well-drained soil in a sunny position. Lavender's mauve-purple flowers bloom from June to September.

• Lavender grows well indoors.

Parts used for liqueur: Flowers (best picked soon after they've blossomed, while in their prime).

LAVENDER BRANDY LIQUEUR

Lavender brandy liqueur is a rich golden colour, with sweet, exotic fragrance and exciting fruit-fresh taste. Alcoholic strength (when brandy of around 40% Vol is used) about 23% alcohol by volume. Stronger brandy produces a more potent liqueur!

*Dried lavender flowers, spices, pure juice and honeys are available from your local health-food stockist.

INGREDIENTS: to make 1 standard-size wine bottle.
Fresh lavender flowers – 3 level tablespoons
   or *dried flowers – 1 level tablespoon
***Pure pineapple juice – 6 fl oz (170ml)**
***Pure lime blossom or mixed blossom honey –**
   4 heaped tablespoons
Nutmeg (ground) – ½ level 5ml teaspoon
Ginger (ground) – ¼ level 5ml teaspoon
Brandy – 17 fl oz (483ml)

Large jar (with tight-fitting lid) – big enough to hold all ingredients, or one empty 1 litre wine, spirit or cider bottle (in which to macerate ingredients) and cork or plastic stopper.

METHOD
   Sterilise (see page 38) and *rinse* utensils before use. To measure fresh lavender flowers (if used), remove and discard pieces of green leaf and stalk and gently press flowers in tablespoon. Lightly rinse fresh lavender flowers in cold water. Warm pineapple juice in small saucepan. Stir in honey, nutmeg and ginger. When dissolved, cover and allow to cool. Place lavender flowers, then brandy and lastly juice-honey mixture in jar or bottle (use a plastic funnel for liquid). Fasten lid or stopper. Store somewhere warm for 10 days. Then strain liqueur through a fine-mesh strainer into a large jug. Squeeze liquid from flowers. Discard solids. Pour the cloudy liqueur through a plastic funnel into an empty wine bottle. Stopper the bottle with a cork or plastic stopper. Store in a cool place for

9 weeks to clear and permit the flavours to blend and mellow. Then syphon or carefully pour the liqueur from its sediment into a large jug; filter (see page 50) liqueur through a plastic funnel into an empty wine or liqueur bottle – fasten a cork or plastic stopper.

Your Lavender Brandy Liqueur is now ready to enjoy, and should continue to improve in quality for a further 9–12 weeks, before achieving peak excellence. Serve at room temperature in liqueur glasses. Cheers!

Lime

LIME, also known as LINDEN (*Tilia europaea* and other trees of the Linden family *Tiliaceae*).

Today lime trees are popularly planted to line roads, and to landscape ornamental settings. The soft, firm and easily carved wood makes handsome furniture, and parts for musical instruments.

For centuries sweethearts declared love for one another beneath the lime tree – sacred to Freyja, the Norse goddess of love. Wine made from the tree's flowers was shared by courting couples as a pledge of undying love.

The lime is a perennial, deciduous (sheds leaves annually) tree of 65–100 feet (20–30 metres) in height. It likes rich, well-drained, moist soil in a sunny position. The lime's sweet-smelling, cream-yellow flowers bloom in clusters in June and July.

Parts used for wine: Flowers (best picked on warm day, when open and fragrant with sweet honey aroma).

LIME FLOWER HERB WINE

Lime flower herb wine develops a glowing cider-gold colour, with sweet honey-rich fragrance and succulent taste – to caress and soothe your senses; enjoyable as an aperitif, table or social wine of about 11.5% alcohol by volume.

Sultanas (dried white grapes) give extra flavour, body and smoothness to this wine and nourish the wine yeast, encouraging maximum efficiency in alcohol production.

*Dried herbs, pure juices and honeys are available from your local health-food stockist. Dried lime flowers (blossom) are also available from home-brew stockists.

INGREDIENTS: to make 1 gallon (4½ litres).
Fresh lime flowers – 1¾ pints (1 litre)
  or *dried flowers (blossom) – 2 oz (56g)
Water – up to 1 gallon (4½ litres)
Granulated sugar *(optional, see below)* **– 1½ lb (680g)**
Tea, strong – ½ cup
Sultanas – 12 oz (340g)
Lemons – 2
***Pure apple juice – 1¾ pints (1 litre)**
Wine yeast – amount recommended by manufacturer

SUGAR-FREE "SECRET" RECIPE (see page 23): To make lime flower herb wine without adding sugar (sucrose) replace the entire quantity of granulated sugar with **1 lb (454g) of *pure lime blossom or acacia blossom honey; and either 2¾ pints (1½ litres) of *pure white grape juice, or ¾ pint (426ml) of wine making concentrated white grape juice.**

METHOD

Sterilise (see page 38) and *rinse* wine making equipment and utensils before use. To measure fresh lime flowers (if used), discard pieces of green leaf and stalk and gently press flowers down in measuring jug. Lightly rinse fresh flowers in cold water. Put fresh flowers or dried flowers in plastic (food grade) bucket. Cover. Warm 1 pint (½ litre) of water in large saucepan. Stir in granulated sugar or pure honey. When dissolved, cover and leave to cool. Make tea, strain and allow to cool, or use strained cold tea from an earlier brew. Discard tea leaves or bag. Rinse sultanas in warm water. Chop or mince sultanas. Extract juice from lemons. Discard pips, pith and peel. Pour pure apple juice, and grape juice (if used), lemon juice, brewed tea, and dissolved sugar or honey into bucket. Add sultanas, wine yeast and cold water to raise the total quantity of liquid to about 7 pints (4 litres). Allow at least 2 inches (51mm) – 4 inches (102mm) at the top of your bucket for the fermentation's initial frothing. Cover. Keep bucket in a warm place for 9 days. Stir twice daily.

After nine days pour or scoop the fermenting wine from its sediment and strain into a narrow-necked 1 gallon (4½ litres) fermentation vessel. Discard solids. Top up to the neck with cold water. Fit cork or rubber bung and air lock filled with water, or sulphite solution (see page 39). Leave in the warm until fermentation is complete; this can take 4–5 weeks at an even temperature of 18°C (64°F).

Fermentation has finished when bubbles have ceased passing through the liquid in the air lock. A wine hydrometer reading (see page 44) of around 0.997 indicates fermentation may have ended. Check your lime flower herb wine tastes dry (non-sweet), is not fizzy on your tongue and is beginning to fall clear from the surface downwards.

When satisfied fermentation has finished, syphon or pour wine from its sediment into a narrow-necked 1 gallon (4½ litre) storage vessel. Top up to the neck with wine of a similar flavour and colour, or cold water. Fit a cork or rubber bung. Store somewhere cool to clear and mature before bottling.

Your lime flavour herb wine should be clear and ready to bottle after about 6 months' storage, though a few months longer improves the wine's quality. When bottled, the wine needs a further 2–3 months to condition and mature before drinking.

Lime flower herb wine achieves peak excellence about 18 months after the fermented wine has been transferred to a storage vessel to clear and mature.

Marigold

MARIGOLD *(Calendula officinalis)*.

The sun-loving marigold can be used to flavour soup, casseroles, salad, stuffings, bread, cake and butter.

According to folklore marigolds are associated with love and clairvoyance, and marigold wine is credited with the power to help open your *inner mind* to clairvoyant perception.

Marigold is an annual plant of around 1¼ feet (0.38m) in height. It likes almost any type of soil in a sunny position. Marigold's orange flowers bloom from June to October.

Parts used for wine and liqueur: Flowers (flower heads. – best picked on a dry day before noon).

MARIGOLD FLOWER HERB WINE

Marigold flower herb wine develops a lovely yellow-gold colour, with a delicate aroma and rich spice-fruit flavour; enjoyable as an aperitif, table or social wine of about 11.5% alcohol by volume.

Sultanas (dried white grapes) give extra flavour, body and smoothness to this wine and nourish the wine yeast, encouraging maximum efficiency in alcohol production.

*Dried herbs, pure juices and honeys are available from your local health-food stockist.

INGREDIENTS: to make 1 gallon (4½ litres).
Fresh marigold flower heads – 1¾ pints (1 litre)
 or *dried heads – 2 oz (56g)
Water – up to 1 gallon (4½ litres)
Granulated sugar (optional, see below) **– 1½ lb (680g)**
Tea, strong – ½ cup
Sultanas – 12 oz (340g)
***Pure orange juice – 1¾ pints (1 litre)**
Wine yeast – amount recommended by manufacturer

SUGAR-FREE "SECRET" RECIPE (see page 23): To make marigold flower herb wine without adding sugar (sucrose) replace the entire quantity of granulated sugar with **1 lb (454g) of *pure orange blossom or lime blossom honey; and either 2¾ pints (1½ litres) of *pure white grape juice, or ¾ pint (426ml) of wine making concentrated white grape juice.**

METHOD
Sterilise (see page 38) and *rinse* wine making equipment and utensils before use. To measure fresh marigold heads (if used), remove and discard pieces of green leaf and stalk and gently press heads in measuring jug. Lightly rinse fresh heads in cold water. Put fresh or dried heads in plastic (food grade) bucket. Cover. Warm 1 pint (½ litre) of water in large saucepan. Stir in granulated sugar or pure honey. When dissolved, cover and leave to cool. Make tea, strain and allow to cool, or use strained cold tea from an earlier brew. Discard tea leaves or bag. Rinse sultanas in warm water. Chop or mince sultanas. Pour pure orange juice and white grape

juice (if used), brewed tea, and dissolved sugar or honey into bucket. Add sultanas, wine yeast and cold water to raise the total quantity of liquid to about 7 pints (4 litres). Allow at least 2 inches (51mm) – 4 inches (102mm) at the top of your bucket for the fermentation's initial frothing. Cover. Keep bucket in a warm place for 9 days. Stir twice daily.

After nine days pour or scoop the fermenting wine from its sediment and strain into a narrow-necked 1 gallon (4½ litres) fermentation vessel. Discard solids. Top up to the neck with cold water. Fit cork or rubber bung and air lock filled with water, or sulphite solution (see page 39). Leave in the warm until fermentation is complete; this can take 4–5 weeks at an even temperature of 18°C (64°F).

Fermentation has finished when bubbles have ceased passing through the liquid in the air lock. A wine hydrometer reading (see page 44) of around 0.997 indicates fermentation may have ended. Check your marigold flower herb wine tastes dry (non-sweet), is not fizzy on your tongue and is beginning to fall clear from the surface downwards.

When satisfied fermentation has finished, syphon or pour wine from its sediment into a narrow-necked 1 gallon (4½ litres) storage vessel. Top up to the neck with wine of a similar flavour and colour, or cold water. Fit a cork or rubber bung. Store somewhere cool to clear and mature before bottling.

Your marigold flower herb wine should be clear and ready to bottle after about 5 months' storage, though a few months longer improves the wine's quality. When bottled, the wine needs a further 2–3 months to condition and mature before drinking.

Marigold flower herb wine achieves peak excellence about 20 months after the fermented wine has

been transferred to a storage vessel to clear and
mature.

MARIGOLD BRANDY LIQUEUR

Marigold brandy liqueur is a radiant honey-gold
colour, with spicy aroma and refreshing full flavour.
Alcoholic strength (when brandy of around 40% Vol
is used) about 23% alcohol by volume. Stronger
brandy produces a more potent liqueur!

*Dried marigold flowers (flower heads), liquorice
root, spices, pure juice and honeys are available from
your local health-food stockist.

INGREDIENTS: to make 1 standard-size wine bottle.
Fresh marigold flower heads – 1 pint (½ litre)
    or *dried heads – 1 oz (28g)
***Pure pineapple juice – 6 fl oz (170ml)**
***Pure lime blossom or orange blossom honey –**
    4 heaped tablespoons
Coriander (ground) – ¼ level 5ml teaspoon
Ginger (ground) – ¼ level 5ml teaspoon
Nutmeg (ground) – ¼ level 5ml teaspoon
***Liquorice root, whole (dried) – 2 of average size –**
    about 5 inches (127mm) long and ¼ inch (6mm) thick
Brandy – 17 fl oz (483ml)

**Large jar (with tight-fitting lid) – big enough to hold
all ingredients, or one empty 1 litre wine, spirit or
cider bottle (in which to macerate ingredients) and
cork or plastic stopper.**

METHOD

Sterilise (see page 38) and *rinse* utensils before use.
To measure fresh marigold heads (if used), remove
and discard pieces of green leaf and stalk and gently

press heads in measuring jug. Lightly rinse fresh heads in cold water. Slice or chop fresh or dried flower heads into slim strips. Warm pineapple juice in small saucepan. Stir in honey, coriander, ginger and nutmeg. When dissolved, cover and allow to cool. Rinse liquorice root in warm water, then break into ½ inch (13mm) pieces and crush with rolling pin or hammer. Place marigold flower strips, liquorice, then brandy and lastly juice-honey mixture in jar or bottle (use a plastic funnel for liquid). Fasten lid or stopper. Store somewhere warm for 10 days. Then strain liqueur through a fine-mesh strainer into a large jug. Squeeze liquid from flower strips and soft liquorice root. Discard solids. Pour the cloudy liqueur through a plastic funnel into an empty wine bottle. Stopper the bottle with a cork or plastic stopper. Store in a cool place for 9 weeks to clear and permit the flavours to blend and mellow. Then syphon or carefully pour the liqueur from its sediment into a large jug; filter (see page 50) liqueur through a plastic funnel into an empty wine or liqueur bottle – fasten a cork or plastic stopper.

Your Marigold Brandy Liqueur is now ready to enjoy, and should continue to improve in quality for a further 9–12 weeks, before achieving peak excellence. Serve at room temperature in liqueur glasses. Cheers!

Marjoram

MARJORAM *(Origanum marjorana),* also known as
SWEET MARJORAM *(Majorana hortensis).*

Oil extracted from sweet marjoram is used in perfumes; toilet waters, beauty lotions and soap. Sweet
marjoram's leaves and flowering tops flavour many
tasty dishes (meat, vegetable, poultry, fish, soup,
salad, stew, sauces, stuffings and bread).

Sweet marjoram, native to warm countries of the
Mediterranean and western Asia, is a naturally perennial plant, but has to be cultivated as an *annual* plant
(outdoors) in colder climates – including Britain.
Sweet Marjoram reaches around 1 foot (0.30m) in
height. It likes moist, medium-rich soil in a sunny
and sheltered position. Sweet marjoram's mauve-purple (also cream-white) flowers bloom from July to
September.

- Marjoram grows well indoors.

Parts used for wine: Leaves (best picked from July
to September, while the plant is flowering).

Please note: Good wine of a slightly less excellent
quality can be made from leaves of the related perennial marjorams: Pot Marjoram *(Origanum* or *Marjorana onites)* and Wild Marjoram, also known as
Wild Oregano *(Origanum vulgare).*

MARJORAM HERB WINE

Marjoram herb wine develops a rich and radiant red colour, with spicy aroma and warm, soothing taste; enjoyable as an aperitif or social wine of about 12.5% alcohol by volume.

Raisins (dried black grapes) give extra flavour, body and smoothness to this wine and nourish the wine yeast, encouraging maximum efficiency in alcohol production.

*Dried herbs, pure juices and honeys are available from your local health-food stockist.

INGREDIENTS: to make 1 gallon (4½ litres).
Fresh marjoram leaves – 1 pint (½ litre)
   or *dried leaves – 1 oz (28g)
Water – up to 1 gallon (4½ litres)
Granulated sugar *(optional, see below)* **– 1½ lb (680g)**
Tea, strong – ½ cup
Raisins – 12 oz (340g)
Lemons – 2
*Pure red grape juice – 1¾ pints (1 litre)
Wine yeast – amount recommended by manufacturer

SUGAR-FREE "SECRET" RECIPE (see page 23): To make marjoram herb wine without adding sugar (sucrose) replace the entire quantity of granulated sugar with **1 lb (454g) of *pure clover or mixed blossom honey; and either 2¾ pints (1½ litres) of *pure red grape juice, or ¾ pint (426ml) of wine making concentrated red grape juice.**

METHOD

Sterilise (see page 38) and *rinse* wine making equipment and utensils before use. To measure fresh marjoram leaves (if used), discard pieces of stalk and

gently press leaves in measuring jug. Lightly rinse
fresh leaves in cold water. Put fresh or dried leaves
in plastic (food grade) bucket. Cover. Warm 1 pint
(½ litre) of water in large saucepan. Stir in granulated
sugar or pure honey. When dissolved, cover and leave
to cool. Make tea, strain and allow to cool, or use
strained cold tea from an earlier brew. Discard tea
leaves or bag. Rinse raisins in warm water. Chop or
mince raisins. Extract juice from lemons. Discard
pips, pith and peel. Pour red grape juice, lemon juice,
brewed tea, and dissolved sugar or honey into bucket.
Add raisins, wine yeast and cold water to raise the
total quantity of liquid to about 7 pints (4 litres).
Allow at least 2 inches (51mm) – 4 inches (102mm)
at the top of your bucket for the fermentation's initial
frothing. Cover. Keep bucket in a warm place for 7
days. Stir twice daily.

After seven days pour or scoop the fermenting wine
from its sediment and strain into a narrow-necked
1 gallon (4½ litres) fermentation vessel. Discard solids.
Top up to the neck with cold water. Fit cork or rubber
bung and air lock filled with water, or sulphite solution (see page 39). Leave in the warm until fermentation is complete; this can take 4–5 weeks at an even
temperature of 18°C (64°F).

Fermentation has finished when bubbles have
ceased passing through the liquid in the air lock. A
wine hydrometer reading (see page 44) of around
0.997 indicates fermentation may have ended. Check
your marjoram herb wine tastes dry (non-sweet), is
not fizzy on your tongue and is beginning to fall clear
from the surface downwards.

When satisfied fermentation has finished, syphon
or pour wine from its sediment into a narrow-necked
one gallon (4½ litres) storage vessel. Top up to the

neck with wine of a similar flavour and colour, or cold water. Fit a cork or rubber bung. Store somewhere cool to clear and mature before bottling.

Your marjoram herb wine should be clear and ready to bottle after about 6 months' storage, though a few months longer improves the wine's quality. When bottled, the wine needs a further 2–3 months to condition and mature before drinking.

Marjoram herb wine achieves peak excellence about 22 months after the fermented wine has been transferred to a storage vessel to clear and mature.

Meadowsweet

MEADOWSWEET *(Filipendula ulmaria)*.

The fragrant meadowsweet – one of the Ancient Druids' sacred herbs – has long been associated with love, peace and gentleness. Meadowsweet's flowers and leaves traditionally scented rooms. They were sewn into sweet-smelling "love sachet" charms, and flavoured alcoholic and non-alcoholic beverages.

Meadowsweet is a perennial plant of 3–5 feet (1– 1½ metres) in height. It likes moist soil, particularly

near fresh water – ponds, streams, rivers.
Meadowsweet's cream flowers bloom from June to
September.

Parts used for wine: Dried leaves, also flowers (fresh
or dried flowers).
Leaves (fresh): For best results, gather *young* fresh
leaves – picked before the plant flowers. Remove
and discard pieces of stalk; dry fresh leaves in a warm
place (see page 29) before use. 5 oz (142g) of fresh
leaves dry to about 1 oz (28g). Drying enhances the
flavour and medicinal value of meadowsweet leaves.
Flowers (fresh): Harvest when open and in full
bloom, at any time during the plant's flowering season
(June–September).

Please note
To make meadowsweet herb wine with dried leaves
and flowers, simply add ½ pint (284ml) of fresh
flowers or ½ oz (14g) of dried flowers to the herb
wine recipe. Meadowsweet flowers add extra fragrance, colour and flavour to the herb wine. Any such
addition is optional, and left to your discretion.

To make meadowsweet herb wine with flowers
only, simply replace the dried leaves in the herb wine
recipe with 1 pint (½ litre) of fresh flowers or 1 oz
(28g) of dried flowers. Proceed with recipe exactly
as specified for meadowsweet herb (leaf) wine.

MEADOWSWEET HERB WINE
Meadowsweet herb (leaf) wine develops a yellow-
bronze colour, with an appetising aroma and delicious
taste; enjoyable as an aperitif, table or social wine
of about 11.5% alcohol by volume.

Sultanas (dried white grapes) give extra flavour,
body and smoothness to this wine and nourish the

wine yeast, encouraging maximum efficiency in
alcohol production.

*Dried herbs, pure juices and honeys are available
from your local health-food stockist.

INGREDIENTS: to make 1 gallon (4½ litres).
*Dried meadowsweet leaves – ¾ oz (21g)
Water – up to 1 gallon (4½ litres)
Granulated sugar *(optional, see below)* **– 1½ lb (680g)**
Tea, strong – ½ cup
Sultanas – 12 oz (340g)
*Pure pineapple juice – 1¾ pints (1 litre)
Wine yeast – amount recommended by manufacturer

SUGAR-FREE "SECRET" RECIPE (see page 23): To
make meadowsweet herb wine without adding sugar
(sucrose) replace the entire quantity of granulated
sugar with **1 lb (454g) of *pure lime blossom or acacia
blossom honey; and either 2¾ pints (1½ litres) of *pure
white grape juice, or ¾ pint (426ml) of wine making
concentrated white grape juice.**

METHOD
Sterilise (see page 38) and *rinse* wine making equipment and utensils before use. Put dried leaves in
plastic (food grade) bucket. Cover. Warm 1 pint
(½ litre) of water in large saucepan. Stir in granulated
sugar or pure honey. When dissolved, cover and leave
to cool. Make tea, strain and allow to cool, or use
strained cold tea from an earlier brew. Discard tea
leaves or bag. Rinse sultanas in warm water. Chop
or mince sultanas. Pour pure pineapple juice, and
grape juice (if used), brewed tea, and dissolved sugar
or honey into bucket. Add sultanas, wine yeast and
cold water to raise the total quantity of liquid to about

7 pints (4 litres). Allow at least 2 inches (51mm) – 4 inches (102mm) at the top of your bucket for the fermentation's initial frothing. Cover. Keep bucket in a warm place for 7 days. Stir twice daily.

After seven days pour or scoop the fermenting wine from its sediment and strain into a narrow-necked 1 gallon (4½ litres) fermentation vessel. Discard solids. Top up to the neck with cold water. Fit cork or rubber bung and air lock filled with water, or sulphite solution (see page 39). Leave in the warm until fermentation is complete; this can take 4–5 weeks at an even temperature of 18°C (64°F).

Fermentation has finished when bubbles have ceased passing through the liquid in the air lock. A wine hydrometer reading (see page 44) of around 0.997 indicates fermentation may have ended. Check your meadowsweet herb wine tastes dry (non-sweet), is not fizzy on your tongue and is beginning to fall clear from the surface downwards.

When satisfied fermentation has finished, syphon or pour wine from its sediment into a narrow-necked 1 gallon (4½ litres) storage vessel. Top up to the neck with wine of a similar flavour and colour, or cold water. Fit a cork or rubber bung. Store somewhere cool to clear and mature before bottling.

Your meadowsweet herb wine should be clear and ready to bottle after about 6 months' storage, though a few months longer improves the wine's quality. When bottled, the wine needs a further 2–3 months to condition and mature before drinking.

Meadowsweet herb wine achieves peak excellence about 20 months after the fermented wine has been transferred to a storage vessel to clear and mature.

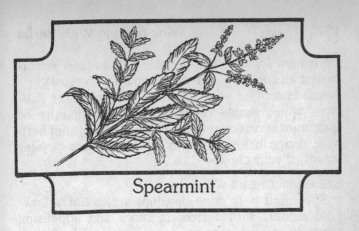

Spearmint

MINT *(Mentha genus, over 20 species).*

The ancient Greeks used mints to make scent, perfume and herbal bath sachets. The Romans added mint to wine, ale and food dishes. Today mint flavours liqueurs (including Crème De Menthe), soup, sauces, salad, vegetables, cream and cottage cheeses; also summer fruit cups and punches, sweets and medicine. Oil from mints is used in scent, perfume, soap and beauty preparations.

A "herb pillow" stuffed with dried mint leaves is a traditional remedy for disturbed or sleepless nights due to colds or influenza.

Popular mints for natural wine making include: Apple Mint *(Mentha rotundifolia);* Orange Mint *(Mentha citrata);* Peppermint *(Mentha piperita);* Pineapple Mint *(Mentha suaveolens);* Spearmint *(Mentha spicata* or *Mentha viridis).*

Mints are perennial plants ranging from 1 foot (0.30m) to 3 feet (1 metre) in height, depending on species. Most mints like moist, rich soil in a shaded position; peppermint prefers a sunny spot. Mints' small flowers (white, lilac, mauve) bloom from July to September.

- Mints grow well indoors.

Parts used for wine and liqueur: Leaves (can be harvested all summer; best collected July–August).
Please note: Use your favourite mint to make delicious wine; simply replace the entire quantity of spearmint leaves recommended in the spearmint herb wine recipe below, with an equal measure of mint leaves of your choice.

SPEARMINT HERB WINE

Spearmint herb wine develops a pleasant yellow-gold colour, with a rich fragrance and appetising flavour; enjoyable as an aperitif or social wine of about 11.5% alcohol by volume.

Sultanas (dried white grapes) give extra flavour, body and smoothness to this wine and nourish the wine yeast, encouraging maximum efficiency in alcohol production.

*Dried herbs, pure juices and honeys are available from your local health-food stockist.

INGREDIENTS: to make 1 gallon (4½ litres).
Fresh spearmint leaves – ¾ pint (426ml)
  or *dried leaves – ¾ oz (21g)
Water – up to 1 gallon (4½ litres)
Granulated sugar *(optional, see below)* **– 1½ lb (680g)**
Tea, strong – ½ cup
Sultanas – 12 oz (340g)
***Pure pineapple juice – 1¾ pints (1 litre)**
Wine yeast – amount recommended by manufacturer

SUGAR-FREE "SECRET" RECIPE (see page 23): To make spearmint herb wine without adding sugar (sucrose) replace the entire quantity of granulated sugar with **1 lb (454g)** of *pure acacia blossom or clover honey; and either **2¾ pints (1½ litres)** of *pure white grape juice, or **¾ pint (426ml)** of wine making concentrated white grape juice.

METHOD

Sterilise (see page 38) and *rinse* wine making equipment and utensils before use. To measure fresh spearmint leaves (if used), discard pieces of stalk and gently press leaves in measuring jug. Lightly rinse fresh leaves in cold water. Put fresh or dried leaves in plastic (food grade) bucket. Cover. Warm 1 pint (½ litre) of water in large saucepan. Stir in granulated sugar or pure honey. When dissolved, cover and leave to cool. Make tea, strain and allow to cool, or use strained cold tea from an earlier brew. Discard tea leaves or bag. Rinse sultanas in warm water. Chop or mince sultanas. Pour pure pineapple juice, and grape juice (if used), brewed tea, and dissolved sugar or honey into bucket. Add sultanas, wine yeast and cold water to raise the total quantity of liquid to about 7 pints (4 litres). Allow at least 2 inches (51mm) – 4 inches (102mm) at the top of your bucket for the fermentation's initial frothing. Cover. Keep bucket in a warm place for 7 days. Stir twice daily.

After seven days pour or scoop the fermenting wine from its sediment and strain into a narrow-necked 1 gallon (4½ litres) fermentation vessel. Discard solids. Top up to the neck with cold water. Fit cork or rubber bung and air lock filled with water, or sulphite solution (see page 39). Leave in the warm until fermentation is complete; this can take 4–5 weeks at an even temperature of 18°C (64°F).

Fermentation has finished when bubbles have ceased passing through the liquid in the air lock. A wine hydrometer reading (see page 44) of around 0.997 indicates fermentation may have ended. Check your spearmint herb wine tastes dry (non-sweet), is not fizzy on your tongue and is beginning to fall clear from the surface downwards.

When satisfied fermentation has finished, syphon

or pour wine from its sediment into a narrow-necked 1 gallon (4½ litres) storage vessel. Top up to the neck with wine of a similar flavour and colour, or cold water. Fit a cork or rubber bung. Store somewhere cool to clear and mature before bottling.

Your spearmint herb wine should be clear and ready to bottle after about 6 months' storage, though a few months longer improves the wine's quality. When bottled, the wine needs a further 2–3 months to condition and mature before drinking.

Spearmint herb wine achieves peak excellence about 20 months after the fermented wine has been transferred to a storage vessel to clear and mature.

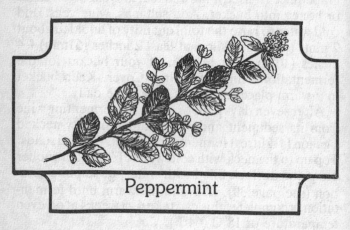

Peppermint

LIQUEUR DE MENTHE

Peppermint liqueur is a glorious green-gold colour, with a superb fragrance and entrancing flavour. Alcoholic strength (when gin or vodka of around 40% Vol is used) about 23% alcohol by volume. Stronger gin or vodka produces a more potent liqueur!

*Dried peppermint leaves, angelica candied stem,

liquorice root, pure juice and honeys are available from your local health-food stockist.

INGREDIENTS: to make 1 standard-size wine bottle.

Fresh peppermint leaves – 7 fl oz (200ml)
  or *dried leaves – 2 level tablespoons
***Pure pineapple juice – 6 fl oz (170ml)**
***Pure lime blossom or acacia blossom honey –**
  4 heaped tablespoons
Fresh angelica stem (cut while plant is flowering, see
  page 55) – 5 oz (142g)
  or *candied stem – 3 oz (85g)
***Liquorice root, whole (dried) – 2 of average size –**
  about 5 inches (127mm) long and ¼ inch (6mm) thick
Gin or vodka – 17 fl oz (483ml)

Large jar (with tight-fitting lid) – big enough to hold all ingredients, or one empty 1 litre wine, spirit or cider bottle (in which to macerate ingredients) and cork or plastic stopper.

METHOD

Sterilise (see page 38) and *rinse* utensils before use. To measure fresh peppermint leaves (if used), remove and discard pieces of stalk and gently press leaves in measuring jug. Lightly rinse fresh leaves in cold water. Warm pineapple juice in small saucepan. Stir in honey. When dissolved, cover and allow to cool. Rinse fresh angelica stem in cold water; slice fresh or candied angelica stem into thin pieces. Rinse liquorice root in warm water, then break into ½ inch (13mm) pieces and crush with rolling pin or hammer. Place peppermint leaves, angelica stem, liquorice, then gin or vodka and lastly juice-honey mixture in jar or bottle (use a plastic funnel for liquid). Fasten lid or stopper. Store somewhere warm for 10 days. Then strain liqueur through a fine-mesh strainer into a large jug. Squeeze liquid from leaves, angelica stem and soft liquorice root. Discard solids. Pour the cloudy liqueur through a plastic funnel into an empty wine bottle. Stopper the bottle with a cork or plastic stopper. Store in a cool place for 9 weeks to clear and permit the flavours to blend and mellow. Then syphon or carefully pour the liqueur from its sediment into a large jug; filter (see page 50) liqueur through a plastic funnel into an empty wine or liqueur bottle – fasten a cork or plastic stopper.

Your Liqueur De Menthe is now ready to enjoy, and should continue to improve in quality for a further 9–12 weeks, before achieving peak excellence. Serve at room temperature in liqueur glasses. Good health!

Nettle

NETTLE *(Urtica dioica)*.

The nutritious common "stinging" nettle, was an important food in ancient times and a popular ingredient in wine and ale. Nettle wine was long considered an arouser of sexual appetite and sure cure for impotence! Anglo-Saxon settlers spun the nettle's stem fibres into yarn and wove fine and coarse cloth, strong ropes and fishing nets. Young nettle shoots, tender tops and leaves make delicious salad, vegetable, soup, stew and stuffings.

Nettle is a perennial plant growing to around 5 feet (1½ metres) in height. It likes rich, moist soil in a sunny position and grows wild in waste places, woods and hedges. Nettle's catkin clusters of small green flowers bloom from June to September.

Parts used for wine: Leaves (best picked when young and pale green, especially April to May – before the plant flowers).

Please note: To avoid nettle stings – wear gloves when gathering leaves; strong scissors are useful.

NETTLE HERB WINE

Nettle herb wine develops a light yellow-green colour, with pleasant aroma and splendid, unique nettle-tang taste; enjoyable as an aperitif or social wine of about 11.5% alcohol by volume.

Sultanas (dried white grapes) give extra flavour, body and smoothness to this wine and nourish the wine yeast, encouraging maximum efficiency in alcohol production.

*Dried herbs, pure juices and honeys are available from your local health-food stockist.

INGREDIENTS: to make 1 gallon (4½ litres).
Fresh nettle leaves – 1¾ pints (1 litre)
   or *dried leaves – 2 oz (56g)
Water – up to 1 gallon (4½ litres)
Granulated sugar (*optional, see below*) **– 1½ lb (680g)**
Tea, strong – ½ cup
Sultanas – 12 oz (340g)
Lemons – 2
***Pure apple juice – 1¾ pints (1 litre)**
Wine yeast – amount recommended by manufacturer

SUGAR-FREE "SECRET" RECIPE (see page 23): To make nettle herb wine without adding sugar (sucrose) replace the entire quantity of granulated sugar with **1 lb (454g) of *pure acacia blossom or mixed blossom honey; and either 2¾ pints (1½ litres) of *pure white grape juice, or ¾ pint (426ml) of wine making concentrated white grape juice.**

METHOD
Sterilise (see page 38) and *rinse* wine making equipment and utensils before use. To measure fresh nettle leaves (if used), discard pieces of stalk and gently press leaves in measuring jug. Lightly rinse fresh leaves in cold water. Put fresh or dried leaves in plastic (food grade) bucket. Cover. Warm 1 pint (½ litre) of water in large saucepan. Stir in granulated sugar or pure honey. When dissolved, cover and leave to cool. Make tea, strain and allow to cool, or use strained cold tea from an earlier brew. Discard tea leaves or bag. Rinse sultanas in warm water. Chop or mince sultanas. Extract juice from lemons. Discard pips, pith and peel. Pour pure apple juice, and grape juice (if used), lemon juice, brewed tea, and dissolved sugar or honey into bucket. Add sultanas, wine yeast

and cold water to raise the total quantity of liquid to about 7 pints (4 litres). Allow at least 2 inches (51mm) – 4 inches (102mm) at the top of your bucket for the fermentation's initial frothing. Cover. Keep bucket in a warm place for 9 days. Stir twice daily.

After nine days pour or scoop the fermenting wine from its sediment and strain into a narrow-necked 1 gallon (4½ litres) fermentation vessel. Discard solids. Top up to the neck with cold water. Fit cork or rubber bung and air lock filled with water, or sulphite solution (see page 39). Leave in the warm until fermentation is complete; this can take 4–5 weeks at an even temperature of 18°C (64°F).

Fermentation has finished when bubbles have ceased passing through the liquid in the air lock. A wine hydrometer reading (see page 44) of around 0.997 indicates fermentation may have ended. Check your nettle herb wine tastes dry (non-sweet), is not fizzy on your tongue and is beginning to fall clear from the surface downwards.

When satisfied fermentation has finished, syphon or pour wine from its sediment into a narrow-necked one gallon (4½ litres) storage vessel. Top up to the neck with wine of a similar flavour and colour, or cold water. Fit a cork or rubber bung. Store somewhere cool to clear and mature before bottling.

Your nettle herb wine should be clear and ready to bottle after about 7 months' storage, though a few months longer improves the wine's quality. When bottled, the wine needs a further 2–3 months to condition and mature before drinking.

Nettle herb wine achieves peak excellence about 22 months after the fermented wine has been transferred to a storage vessel to clear and mature.

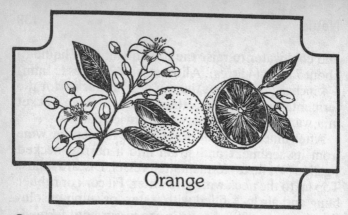

Orange

ORANGE *(Citrus genus, several species)*.

Orange evergreen small trees or shrubs are commercially cultivated in countries that enjoy a warm, temperate or subtropical climate, ranging from Africa to Spain, and including Argentina, Australia, Brazil, India, Israel, Italy, Japan, Mexico, Morocco and parts of the U.S.A.

Oranges (also orange flowers) contribute flavour to commercial liqueurs (including Alkermes, Cointreau, Grand Marnier, Strega, and Van Der Hum).

Orange juice and peel have many culinary uses and flavour bread, cake, custard, ice cream, pies, pudding, sauce, sherbet and sweets.

Orange flowers are used to make orange flower water, a once widely popular ladies' general tonic.

Parts used for wine and liqueur: Flowers (best bought dried from your local health-food or home-brew stockist – unless you grow your own orange trees) and pure orange juice.

ORANGE FLOWER HERB WINE

Orange flower herb wine develops an attractive gold-amber colour, with an appetising full citrus fragrance and mouth-watering taste; enjoyable as an

140

aperitif, table or social wine of about 11.5% alcohol by volume.

Sultanas (dried white grapes) give extra flavour, body and smoothness to this wine and nourish the wine yeast, encouraging maximum efficiency in alcohol production.

*Dried herbs, pure juices and honeys are available from your local health-food stockist. Dried orange flowers (blossom) are also available from home-brew stockists.

INGREDIENTS: to make 1 gallon (4½ litres).
Fresh orange flowers – 1¾ pints (1 litre)
** or *dried flowers (blossom) – 2 oz (56g)**
Water – up to 1 gallon (4½ litres)
Granulated sugar *(optional, see below)* **– 1½ lb (680g)**
Tea, strong – ½ cup
Sultanas – 12 oz (340g)
***Pure orange juice – 1¾ pints (1 litre)**
Wine yeast – amount recommended by manufacturer

SUGAR-FREE "SECRET" RECIPE (see page 23): To make orange flower herb wine without adding sugar (sucrose) replace the entire quantity of granulated sugar with **1 lb (454g) of *pure orange blossom or lime blossom honey; and either 2¾ pints (1½ litres) of *pure white grape juice, or ¾ pint (426ml) of wine making concentrated white grape juice.**

METHOD
Sterilise (see page 38) and *rinse* wine making equipment and utensils before use. To measure fresh orange flowers (if used), discard pieces of green leaf and stalk and gently press flowers in measuring jug. Lightly rinse fresh flowers in cold water. Put fresh

or dried flowers in plastic (food grade) bucket. Cover. Warm 1 pint (½ litre) of water in large saucepan. Stir in granulated sugar or pure honey. When dissolved, cover and leave to cool. Make tea, strain and allow to cool, or use strained cold tea from an earlier brew. Discard tea leaves or bag. Rinse sultanas in warm water. Chop or mince sultanas. Pour pure orange juice and white grape juice (if used), brewed tea, and dissolved sugar or honey into bucket. Add sultanas, wine yeast and cold water to raise the total quantity of liquid to about 7 pints (4 litres). Allow at least 2 inches (51mm) – 4 inches (102mm) at the top of your bucket for the fermentation's initial frothing. Cover. Keep bucket in a warm place for 9 days. Stir twice daily.

After nine days pour or scoop the fermenting wine from its sediment and strain into a narrow-necked 1 gallon (4½ litres) fermentation vessel. Discard solids. Top up to the neck with cold water. Fit cork or rubber bung and air lock filled with water, or sulphite solution (see page 39). Leave in the warm until fermentation is complete; this can take 4–5 weeks at an even temperature of 18°C (64°F).

Fermentation has finished when bubbles have ceased passing through the liquid in the air lock. A wine hydrometer reading (see page 44) of around 0.997 indicates fermentation may have ended. Check your orange flower herb wine tastes dry (non-sweet), is not fizzy on your tongue and is beginning to fall clear from the surface downwards.

When satisfied fermentation has finished, syphon or pour wine from its sediment into a narrow-necked 1 gallon (4½ litres) storage vessel. Top up to the neck with wine of a similar flavour and colour, or cold water. Fit a cork or rubber bung. Store somewhere cool to clear and mature before bottling.

Your orange flower herb wine should be clear and ready to bottle after about 6 months' storage, though a few months longer improves the wine's quality. When bottled, the wine needs a further 2–3 months to condition and mature before drinking.

Orange flower herb wine achieves peak excellence about 18 months after the fermented wine has been transferred to a storage vessel to clear and mature.

ORANGE BRANDY LIQUEUR

Orange brandy liqueur glows a deep amber colour, with delicious flower fragrance and fiery-warm herb-spice taste. Alcoholic strength (when brandy of around 40% Vol is used) about 23% alcohol by volume. Stronger brandy produces a more potent liqueur!

*Dried orange flowers (blossom), spices, pure juice and honeys are available from your local health-food stockist. Dried orange flowers (blossom) are also available from home-brew stockists.

INGREDIENTS: to make 1 standard-size wine bottle.
Fresh orange flowers – ½ pint (284ml)
   or *dried flowers (blossom) – ½ oz (14g)
***Pure orange juice – 6 fl oz (170ml)**
***Pure orange blossom or lime blossom honey –**
   4 heaped tablespoons
Cinnamon (ground) – ¼ level 5ml teaspoon
Coriander (ground) – ¼ level 5ml teaspoon
Ginger (ground) – ¼ level 5ml teaspoon
Clove (whole) – 1
Brandy – 17 fl oz (483ml)

Large jar (with tight-fitting lid) – big enough to hold all ingredients, or one empty 1 litre wine, spirit or cider bottle (in which to macerate ingredients) and cork or plastic stopper.

METHOD

Sterilise (see page 38) and *rinse* utensils before use. To measure fresh orange flowers (if used), remove and discard pieces of green leaf and stalk and gently press flowers in measuring jug. Lightly rinse fresh flowers in cold water. Warm orange juice in small saucepan. Stir in honey, cinnamon, coriander and ginger. When dissolved, cover and allow to cool. Place orange flowers, clove, then brandy and lastly juice-honey mixture in jar or bottle (use a plastic funnel for liquid). Fasten lid or stopper. Store somewhere warm for 10 days. Then strain liqueur through a fine-mesh strainer into a large jug. Squeeze liquid from flowers. Discard solids. Pour the cloudy liqueur through a plastic funnel into an empty wine bottle. Stopper the bottle with a cork or plastic stopper. Store in a cool place for 9 weeks to clear and permit the flavours to blend and mellow. Then syphon or carefully pour the liqueur from its sediment into a large jug; filter (see page 50) liqueur through a plastic funnel into an empty wine or liqueur bottle – fasten a cork or plastic stopper.

Your Orange Brandy Liqueur is now ready to enjoy, and should continue to improve in quality for a further 9–12 weeks, before achieving peak excellence. Serve at room temperature in liqueur glasses. Good health!

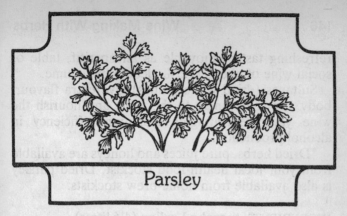

Parsley

PARSLEY *(Petroselinum crispum* or *Petroselinum sativum).*

Parsley has been cultivated for medicinal and culinary use for over 2,000 years. Curly or common cultivated parsley is a nutritious and flavoursome addition to soup, salad, stew, vegetables, sauces and stuffings. Parsley – the principal ingredient of *bouquet garni* and *fines herbes* – makes a delightful and delicious garnish.

Parsley is a biennial plant (often cultivated as an annual) of around 9 inches (0.23m) in height. It likes moist, rich soil in a sunny or shaded position. Parsley's small green-yellow flowers develop in the plant's second year of growth and bloom from June to August.

- Parsley grows well indoors.

Parts used for wine: Leaves (can be harvested from young plants all summer, especially good in early summer. Aim to collect leaves before the plant flowers).

PARSLEY HERB WINE

Parsley herb wine develops a bright gold-green colour, with a unique fresh fragrance and lovely

refreshing taste; enjoyable as an aperitif, table or
social wine of about 11.5% alcohol by volume.

Sultanas (dried white grapes) give extra flavour,
body and smoothness to this wine and nourish the
wine yeast, encouraging maximum efficiency in
alcohol production.

*Dried herbs, pure juices and honeys are available
from your local health-food stockist. Dried parsley
is also available from home-brew stockists.

INGREDIENTS: to make 1 gallon (4½ litres).
Fresh parsley leaves – 3½ pints (2 litres)
  or *dried leaves – 2 oz (56g)
Water – up to 1 gallon (4½ litres)
Granulated sugar *(optional, see below)* **– 1½ lb (680g)**
Tea, strong – ½ cup
Sultanas – 12 oz (340g)
***Pure pineapple juice – 1¾ pints (1 litre)**
Wine yeast – amount recommended by manufacturer

SUGAR-FREE "SECRET" RECIPE (see page 23): To
make parsley herb wine without adding sugar (sucrose) replace the entire quantity of granulated sugar
with **1 lb (454g)** of *pure lime blossom or orange blossom honey; and either **2¾ pints (1½ litres)** of *pure
white grape juice, or **¾ pint (426ml)** of wine making
concentrated white grape juice.

METHOD
Sterilise (see page 38) and *rinse* wine making equipment and utensils before use. To measure fresh
parsley leaves (if used), strip leaves from stalk; discard pieces of stalk and gently press leaves in measuring jug. Lightly rinse fresh leaves in cold water. Put
fresh or dried leaves in plastic (food grade) bucket.
Cover. Warm 1 pint (½ litre) of water in large sauce-

pan. Stir in granulated sugar or pure honey. When dissolved, cover and leave to cool. Make tea, strain and allow to cool, or use strained cold tea from an earlier brew. Discard tea leaves or bag. Rinse sultanas in warm water. Chop or mince sultanas. Pour pine-apple juice, and grape juice (if used), brewed tea, and dissolved sugar or honey into bucket. Add sultanas, wine yeast and cold water to raise the total quantity of liquid to about 7 pints (4 litres). Allow at least 2 inches (51mm) – 4 inches (102mm) at the top of your bucket for the fermentation's initial frothing. Cover. Keep bucket in a warm place for 7 days. Stir twice daily.

After seven days pour or scoop the fermenting wine from its sediment and strain into a narrow-necked 1 gallon (4½ litres) fermentation vessel. Discard solids. Top up to the neck with cold water. Fit cork or rubber bung and air lock filled with water, or sulphite solu-tion (see page 39). Leave in the warm until fermen-tation is complete; this can take 4–5 weeks at an even temperature of 18°C (64°F).

Fermentation has finished when bubbles have ceased passing through the liquid in the air lock. A wine hydrometer reading (see page 44) of around 0.997 indicates fermentation may have ended. Check your parsley herb wine tastes dry (non-sweet), is not fizzy on your tongue and is beginning to fall clear from the surface downwards.

When satisfied fermentation has finished, syphon or pour wine from its sediment into a narrow-necked 1 gallon (4½ litres) storage vessel. Top up to the neck with wine of a similar flavour and colour, or cold water. Fit a cork or rubber bung. Store somewhere cool to clear and mature before bottling.

Your parsley herb wine should be clear and ready

to bottle after about 6 months' storage, though a few months longer improves the wine's quality. When bottled, the wine needs a further 2–3 months to condition and mature before drinking.

Parsley herb wine achieves peak excellence about 20 months after the fermented wine has been transferred to a storage vessel to clear and mature.

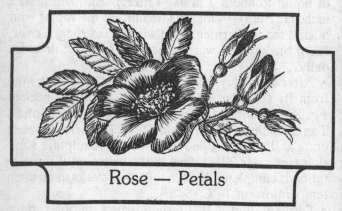

Rose — Petals

ROSE (genus *Rosa*, family: *Rosaceae* – over 200 species!).

Oil from rose petals is used to enhance the flavour and aroma of commercial liqueurs. Rose petals, ancient symbols of love and romance, also provide oil for perfumes, scent, beauty lotions and ointments. Rose petals can flavour many scrumptious foods, including: butter, honey, jam, jelly, salad, Turkish Delight, yoghurt etc.

Rose-hips contain vitamins A, B, E and are extremely rich in vitamin C. Rose-hips are used in the manufacture of rose-hip syrup.

Rose shrubs and vines are perennial and generally

favour firm, rich, well-drained soil in a sunny position. Roses' beautiful and fragrant flowers – orange, pink, red, white, yellow – bloom from around May to August, depending on species and location.

Parts used for wine and liqueur: Petals (best gathered on a dry day before noon) and hips (harvest when ripe – between late August and November).

ROSE PETAL ROSÉ

Rose petal rosé develops a passionate red-rosé colour, with an intoxicating, sensuous fragrance and fresh, fruity taste; enjoyable as an aperitif, table or social wine of about 12.5% alcohol by volume.

Sultanas (dried white grapes) give extra flavour, body and smoothness to this wine and nourish the wine yeast, encouraging maximum efficiency in alcohol production.

*Dried herbs, pure juices and honeys are available from your local health-food stockist. Dried rose petals are also available from home-brew stockists.

INGREDIENTS: to make 1 gallon (4½ litres).
Fresh rose petals (single or mixed colours) – 1¾ pints (1 litre)
or *dried petals – 2 oz (56g)
Water – up to 1 gallon (4½ litres)
Granulated sugar *(optional, see below)* **– 1½ lb (680g)**
Tea, strong – ½ cup
Sultanas – 12 oz (340g)
Lemons – 2
***Pure red grape juice – 1¾ pints (1 litre)**
Wine yeast – amount recommended by manufacturer

SUGAR-FREE "SECRET" RECIPE (see page 23): To make rose petal rosé without adding sugar (sucrose) replace the entire quantity of granulated sugar with **1 lb (454g) of *pure orange blossom or lime blossom honey; and either 2¾ pints (1½ litres) of *pure white grape juice, or ¾ pint (426ml) of wine making concentrated white grape juice.**

METHOD

Sterilise (see page 38) and *rinse* wine making equipment and utensils before use. To measure fresh rose petals (if used), gently press petals in measuring jug. Lightly rinse fresh petals in cold water. Put fresh petals or dried petals in plastic (food grade) bucket. Cover. Warm 1 pint (½ litre) of water in large saucepan. Stir in granulated sugar or pure honey. When dissolved, cover and leave to cool. Make tea, strain and allow to cool, or use strained cold tea from an earlier brew. Discard tea leaves or bag. Rinse sultanas in warm water. Chop or mince sultanas. Extract juice from lemons. Discard pips, pith and peel. Pour pure red grape juice and white grape juice (if used), lemon juice, brewed tea, and dissolved sugar or honey into bucket. Add sultanas, wine yeast and cold water to raise the total quantity of liquid to about 7 pints (4 litres). Allow at least 2 inches (51mm) – 4 inches (102mm) at the top of your bucket for the fermentation's initial frothing. Cover. Keep bucket in a warm place for 9 days. Stir twice daily.

After nine days pour or scoop the fermenting wine from its sediment and strain into a narrow-necked 1 gallon (4½ litres) fermentation vessel. Discard solids. Top up to the neck with cold water. Fit cork or rubber bung and air lock filled with water, or sulphite solution (see page 39). Leave in the warm until fermen-

tation is complete; this can take 4–5 weeks at an even temperature of 18°C (64°F).

Fermentation has finished when bubbles have ceased passing through the liquid in the air lock. A wine hydrometer reading (see page 44) of around 0.997 indicates fermentation may have ended. Check your rose petal rosé tastes dry (non-sweet), is not fizzy on your tongue and is beginning to fall clear from the surface downwards.

When satisfied fermentation has finished, syphon or pour wine from its sediment into a narrow-necked 1 gallon (4½ litres) storage vessel. Top up to the neck with wine of a similar flavour and colour, or cold water. Fit a cork or rubber bung. Store somewhere cool to clear and mature before bottling.

Your rose petal rosé should be clear and ready to bottle after about 6 months' storage, though a few months longer improves the wine's quality. When bottled, the wine needs a further 2–3 months to condition and mature before drinking.

Rose petal rosé achieves peak excellence about 22 months after the fermented wine has been transferred to a storage vessel to clear and mature.

Rose-hips

ROSE BRANDY LIQUEUR

Rose brandy liqueur is a tantalising red-gold colour
– with a sweet fragrance, voluptuous body and elec-
trifying flavour. Alcoholic strength (when brandy of
around 40% Vol is used) about 23% alcohol by
volume. Stronger brandy produces a more potent
liqueur!

*Dried rose petals, hips, spices, pure juice and
honeys are available from your local health-food
stockist. Dried rose petals and hips are also available
from home-brew stockists.

INGREDIENTS: to make 1 standard-size wine bottle.
Dried rose-hips – 1 oz (28g)
  or fresh rose-hips – 2 oz (56g)
**Fresh rose petals (single or mixed colours) – ½ pint
  (284ml) or *dried petals – ½ oz (14g)**
Pure red grape juice – 6 fl oz (170ml)
**Pure clover or mixed blossom honey – 4 heaped
  tablespoons**
Nutmeg (ground) – ½ level 5ml teaspoon
Pure lemon juice – 2 level 5ml teaspoons
Cloves (whole) – 2
Brandy – 17 fl oz (483ml)

Large jar (with tight-fitting lid) – big enough to hold all ingredients, or one empty 1 litre wine, spirit or cider bottle (in which to macerate ingredients) and cork or plastic stopper.

METHOD

Sterilise (see page 38) and *rinse* utensils before use. Rinse dried rose-hips (if used) in warm water; then soak dried hips in cold water for 24 hours before use. To measure fresh rose petals (if used), gently press petals in measuring jug. Remove and discard pieces of stalk from fresh rose-hips. Lightly rinse fresh rose petals or fresh hips in cold water. Warm grape juice in small saucepan. Stir in honey, nutmeg and lemon juice. When dissolved, cover and allow to cool. Slice or chop in half each rose-hip. Place rose petals, hips, cloves, then brandy and lastly juice-honey mixture in jar or bottle (use a plastic funnel for liquid). Fasten lid or stopper. Store somewhere warm for 10 days. Then strain liqueur through a fine-mesh strainer into a large jug. Squeeze liquid from petals and hips. Discard solids. Pour the cloudy liqueur through a plastic funnel into an empty wine bottle. Stopper the bottle with a cork or plastic stopper. Store in a cool place for 9 weeks to clear and permit the flavours to blend and mellow. Then syphon or carefully pour the liqueur from its sediment into a large jug; filter (see page 50) liqueur through a plastic funnel into an empty wine or liqueur bottle – fasten a cork or plastic stopper.

Your Rose Brandy Liqueur is now ready to enjoy, and should continue to improve in quality for a further 9–12 weeks, before achieving peak excellence. Serve at room temperature in liqueur glasses. Cheers!

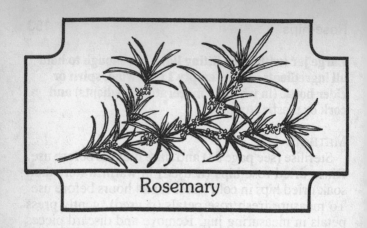

Rosemary

ROSEMARY *(Rosmarinus officinalis)*.

Oil extracted from rosemary flowers (also leaves) is used in perfumes, beauty lotions, shampoo, toilet waters, eau-de-Cologne and facial skin tonics (to prevent or reduce wrinkles!).

Rosemary leaves flavour many delicious foods, including: meat, poultry, stuffings, sauces, seafood, stews, vegetables, salad, soup, cream and cottage cheeses etc.

Rosemary is the principal ingredient in Queen Donna Izabella's *"Elixir of Youth"*, a legendary fourteenth-century Hungarian alchemical liqueur. It worked rejuvenating wonders for the ageing but still sprightly, independent and attractive Queen Donna Izabella who, at seventy-two, refused the infatuated King of Poland's proposal of marriage!

Rosemary is a perennial evergreen shrub of around 5 feet (1½ metres) in height. It likes light, dry, well-drained soil in a sunny and sheltered position. Rosemary's pale blue flowers bloom in April and May.

● Rosemary grows well indoors.

154

Parts used for wine: Leaves (can be picked at any time of year), or flowers (best picked in May).

Please note: An equally excellent and fragrant wine can be made using rosemary flowers – 1 pint (½ litre) of fresh flowers or 1 oz (28g) of dried flowers – in place of the rosemary leaves used in the recipe below.

ROSEMARY HERB WINE

Rosemary herb (leaf) wine develops a light yellow-gold colour with sweet scented fragrance and romantic, spiky-spice and fruit taste; enjoyable as an aperitif or social wine of about 11.5% alcohol by volume.

Sultanas (dried white grapes) give extra flavour, body and smoothness to this wine and nourish the wine yeast, encouraging maximum efficiency in alcohol production.

*Dried herbs, pure juices and honeys are available from your local health-food stockist.

INGREDIENTS: to make 1 gallon (4½ litres).
Fresh rosemary leaves – 1 heaped tablespoon
   or *dried leaves – 1 level tablespoon
Water – up to 1 gallon (4½ litres)
Granulated sugar *(optional, see below)* **– 1½ lb (680g)**
Tea, strong – ½ cup
Sultanas – 12 oz (340g)
Lemons – 2
***Pure apple juice – 1¾ pints (1 litre)**
Wine yeast – amount recommended by manufacturer

SUGAR-FREE "SECRET" RECIPE (see page 23): To make rosemary herb wine without adding sugar (sucrose) replace the entire quantity of granulated sugar with **1 lb (454g) of *pure acacia blossom or orange blossom honey; and either 2¾ pints (1½ litres) of *pure white grape juice, or ¾ pint (426ml) of wine making concentrated white grape juice.**

METHOD

Sterilise (see page 38) and *rinse* wine making equipment and utensils before use. To measure fresh rosemary leaves (if used), discard pieces of stalk and gently press leaves in tablespoon. Lightly rinse fresh leaves in cold water. Put fresh or dried leaves in plastic (food grade) bucket. Cover. Warm 1 pint (½ litre) of water in large saucepan. Stir in granulated sugar or pure honey. When dissolved, cover and leave to cool. Make tea, strain and allow to cool, or use strained cold tea from an earlier brew. Discard tea leaves or bag. Rinse sultanas in warm water. Chop or mince sultanas. Extract juice from lemons. Discard pips, pith and peel. Pour pure apple juice, and grape juice (if used), lemon juice, brewed tea, and dissolved sugar or honey into bucket. Add sultanas, wine yeast and cold water to raise the total quantity of liquid to about 7 pints (4 litres). Allow at least 2 inches (51mm) – 4 inches (102mm) at the top of your bucket for the fermentation's initial frothing. Cover. Keep bucket in a warm place for 7 days. Stir twice daily.

After seven days pour or scoop the fermenting wine from its sediment and strain into a narrow-necked 1 gallon (4½ litres) fermentation vessel. Discard solids. Top up to the neck with cold water. Fit cork or rubber bung and air lock filled with water, or sulphite solution (see page 39). Leave in the warm until fermen-

tation is complete; this can take 4–5 weeks at an even temperature of 18°C (64°F).

Fermentation has finished when bubbles have ceased passing through the liquid in the air lock. A wine hydrometer reading (see page 44) of around 0.997 indicates fermentation may have ended. Check your rosemary herb wine tastes dry (non-sweet), is not fizzy on your tongue and is beginning to fall clear from the surface downwards.

When satisfied fermentation has finished, syphon or pour wine from its sediment into a narrow-necked 1 gallon (4½ litres) storage vessel. Top up to the neck with wine of a similar flavour and colour, or cold water. Fit a cork or rubber bung. Store somewhere cool to clear and mature before bottling.

Your rosemary herb wine should be clear and ready to bottle after about 6 months' storage, though a few months longer improves the wine's quality. When bottled, the wine needs a further 2–3 months to condition and mature before drinking.

Rosemary herb wine achieves peak excellence about 20 months after the fermented wine has been transferred to a storage vessel to clear and mature.

Sage

SAGE *(Salvia officinalis)*.

Since ancient times, sage has been regarded as one of the most beneficial and medicinally valuable herbs. Sage derives its generic name – *Salvia* – from the Latin *salvare,* meaning to save (cure). The Romans praised sage as a god-given blessing. Modern Chinese herbalists rank sage alongside ginseng as a herbal miracle worker!

Oil from sage is used in perfumes and to scent soap. Sage leaves flavour many foods and stuffings.

Sage is a perennial, evergreen small bush of around 2½ feet (0.75m) in height. It likes dry, well-drained soil in a sunny position. Sage's blue-purple or white flowers bloom from June to August.

● Sage grows well indoors.

Parts used for wine: Leaves (can be gathered from June to September; they are best collected in June and July – pick broader leaves first).

SAGE HERB WINE

Sage herb wine develops a bright gold colour, with rich fragrance and enlivening taste; enjoyable as an aperitif or social wine of about 12.5% alcohol by volume.

Sultanas (dried white grapes) give extra flavour, body and smoothness to this wine and nourish the wine yeast, encouraging maximum efficiency in alcohol production.

*Dried herbs, pure juices and honeys are available from your local health-food stockist.

INGREDIENTS: to make 1 gallon (4½ litres).
Fresh sage leaves – ¾ pint (426ml)
   or *dried leaves – ¾ oz (21g)
Water – up to 1 gallon (4½ litres)
Granulated sugar (optional, see below) **1½ lb (680g)**
Tea, strong – ½ cup
Sultanas – 12 oz (340g)
Lemons – 2
***Pure white grape juice – 1¾ pints (1 litre)**
Wine yeast – amount recommended by manufacturer

SUGAR-FREE "SECRET" RECIPE (see page 23): To make sage herb wine without adding sugar (sucrose) replace the entire quantity of granulated sugar with **1 lb (454g) of *pure acacia blossom or mixed blossom honey; and either 2¾ pints (1½ litres) of *pure white grape juice, or ¾ pint (426ml) of wine making concentrated white grape juice.**

METHOD
Sterilise (see page 38) and *rinse* wine making equipment and utensils before use. To measure fresh sage leaves (if used), discard pieces of stalk and gently press leaves in measuring jug. Lightly rinse fresh leaves in cold water. Put fresh or dried leaves in plastic (food grade) bucket. Cover. Warm 1 pint

(½ litre) or water in large saucepan. Stir in granulated sugar or pure honey. When dissolved, cover and leave to cool. Make tea, strain and allow to cool, or use strained cold tea from an earlier brew. Discard tea leaves or bag. Rinse sultanas in warm water. Chop or mince sultanas. Extract juice from lemons. Discard pips, pith and peel. Pour white grape juice, lemon juice, brewed tea, and dissolved sugar or honey into bucket. Add sultanas, wine yeast and cold water to raise the total quantity of liquid to about 7 pints (4 litres). Allow at least 2 inches (51mm) – 4 inches (102mm) at the top of your bucket for the fermentation's initial frothing. Cover. Keep bucket in a warm place for 7 days. Stir twice daily.

After seven days pour or scoop the fermenting wine from its sediment and strain into a narrow-necked 1 gallon (4½ litres) fermentation vessel. Discard solids. Top up to the neck with cold water. Fit cork or rubber bung and air lock filled with water, or sulphite solution (see page 39). Leave in the warm until fermentation is complete; this can take 4–5 weeks at an even temperature of 18°C (64°F).

Fermentation has finished when bubbles have ceased passing through the liquid in the air lock. A wine hydrometer reading (see page 44) of around 0.997 indicates fermentation may have ended. Check your sage herb wine tastes dry (non-sweet), is not fizzy on your tongue and is beginning to fall clear from the surface downwards.

When satisfied fermentation has finished, syphon or pour wine from its sediment into a narrow-necked 1 gallon (4½ litres) storage vessel. Top up to the neck with wine of a similar flavour and colour, or cold water. Fit a cork or rubber bung. Store somewhere cool to clear and mature before bottling.

Your sage herb wine should be clear and ready to bottle after about 6 months' storage, though a few months longer improves the wine's quality. When bottled, the wine needs a further 2–3 months to condition and mature before drinking.

Sage herb wine achieves peak excellence about 20 months after the fermented wine has been transferred to a storage vessel to clear and mature.

Sloe

SLOE, also known as BLACKTHORN *(Prunus spinosa)*.

The sloe or blackthorn is a dense, thorny shrub which grows in hedgerows, woods and scrubland. The shrub can reach 12 feet (3.6m) in height; its snow-white flowers bloom from April to May.

The small, round blue-black berries *(sloes)* are the direct ancestor of today's cultivated plum, and are used to make jelly and Sloe-Gin.

Parts used for liqueur: Berries (sloes) – pick when ripe "soft" and easily removed from shrub, best collected from September to November.

SLOE PINK GIN LIQUEUR

Sloe pink gin liqueur is an attractive pink-red colour, with a smooth honey-grape savour and unique, biting flavour. Alcoholic strength (when gin of around 40% Vol is used) about 23% alcohol by volume. Stronger gin produces a more potent liqueur!

*Dried sloes, spices, pure juice and honeys are available from your local health-food stockist. Dried sloes are also available from home-brew stockists.

INGREDIENTS: to make 1 standard-size wine bottle.
*Dried sloes – 2 oz (57g)
   or fresh sloes – 4 oz (113g)
*Pure red grape juice – 6 fl oz (170ml)
*Pure mixed blossom or clover honey –
   4 heaped tablespoons
Coriander (ground) – ¼ level 5ml teaspoon
Nutmeg (ground) – ½ level 5ml teaspoon
Pure lemon juice – 2 level 5ml teaspoons
Clove (whole) – 1
Gin – 17 fl oz (483ml)

Large jar (with tight-fitting lid) – big enough to hold all ingredients, or one empty 1 litre wine, spirit or cider bottle (in which to macerate ingredients) and cork or plastic stopper.

METHOD

Sterilise (see page 38) and *rinse* utensils before use. Rinse dried sloes (if used) in warm water; then soak dried sloes in cold water for 24 hours before use.

Remove and discard fresh sloe stalks. Lightly rinse fresh sloes in cold water. Warm grape juice in small saucepan. Stir in honey, coriander, nutmeg and lemon juice. When dissolved, cover and allow to cool. Prick fresh or dried (soaked and softened) sloes several times with a sharp sewing-needle (or similar instrument). Place sloes, clove, then gin and lastly juice-honey mixture in jar or bottle (use a plastic funnel for liquid). Fasten lid or stopper. Store somewhere warm for 10 days. Then strain liqueur through a fine-mesh strainer into a large jug. Squeeze liquid from sloes. Discard solids. Pour the cloudy liqueur through a plastic funnel into an empty wine bottle. Stopper the bottle with a cork or plastic stopper. Store in a cool place for 9 weeks to clear and permit the flavours to blend and mellow. Then syphon or carefully pour the liqueur from its sediment into a large jug; filter (see page 50) liqueur through a plastic funnel into an empty wine or liqueur bottle – fasten a cork or plastic stopper.

Your Sloe Pink Gin Liqueur is now ready to enjoy, and should continue to improve in quality for a further 9–12 weeks, before achieving peak excellence. Serve at room temperature in liqueur glasses. Cheers!

Thyme

THYME *(Thymus vulgaris)*.

The ancient Greeks burned sweet-smelling thyme as incense to purify and scent temples for worship. Folklore credits thyme with special spiritually protective properties.

Oil from thyme is a prime ingredient in commercial liqueurs (including Bénédictine, and Frigola – from the Balearic Islands), and in French perfumes. Bees love thyme, and Sicilian *thyme honey* is renowned world-wide for its superb taste.

Thyme flavours many foods: including meat, poultry, fish, pasta, vegetables, salad, coleslaw, soup, cottage and cream cheeses, and butter. A "herb pillow" stuffed with dried thyme is a traditional remedy for insomnia and safeguard against nightmares!

Thyme is a perennial plant of around 9 inches (0.23m) in height. It likes dry, light, well-drained soil in a sunny position. Thyme's purple-pink flowers bloom from June to September.

- Thyme grows well indoors.

Parts used for wine and liqueur: Leaves (gather any time from June to September). Thyme flowers may

164

be used in addition to leaves, bestowing extra fragrance, colour and flavour to thyme wine or liqueur. Add 1 level *table*spoon of fresh flowers, or ½ level *table*spoon of dried flowers to either the herb wine or liqueur recipe. Any such addition is optional, and left to your discretion.

Please note: Good quality wine and liqueur can also be made from the leaves of Lemon Thyme *(Thymus x citriodorus)* and Wild Thyme *(Thymus drucei)*. Lemon or Wild Thyme *flowers* may be used in addition to leaves, as detailed above.

THYME HERB WINE
   Thyme *(Thymus vulgaris)* herb (leaf) wine develops a warm red colour, with a fruity-spice fragrance and a fabulous full-flavoured taste; enjoyable as an aperitif, table or social wine of about 12.5% alcohol by volume.
   Raisins (dried black grapes) give extra flavour, body and smoothness to this wine and nourish the wine yeast, encouraging maximum efficiency in alcohol production.
   *Dried herbs, pure juices and honeys are available from your local health-food stockist.

INGREDIENTS: to make 1 gallon (4½ litres).
Fresh thyme leaves – ¾ pint (426ml)
   or *dried leaves – ¾ oz (21g)
Water – up to 1 gallon (4½ litres)
Granulated sugar *(optional, see below)* **– 1½ lb (680g)**
Tea, strong – ½ cup
Raisins – 12 oz (340g)
Lemons – 2
***Pure red grape juice – 1¾ pints (1 litre)**
Wine yeast – amount recommended by manufacturer

SUGAR-FREE "SECRET" RECIPE (see page 23): To
make thyme herb wine without adding sugar (sucrose)
replace the entire quantity of granulated sugar with
**1 lb (454g) of *pure clover or mixed blossom honey,
or thyme honey; and either 2¾ pints (1½ litres) of
*pure red grape juice, or ¾ pint (426ml) of wine
making concentrated red grape juice.**

METHOD

Sterilise (see page 38) and *rinse* wine making equipment and utensils before use. To measure fresh thyme
leaves (if used), discard pieces of stalk and gently
press leaves in measuring jug. Lightly rinse fresh
leaves in cold water. Put fresh or dried leaves in
plastic (food grade) bucket. Cover. Warm 1 pint
(½ litre) of water in large saucepan. Stir in granulated
sugar or pure honey. When dissolved, cover and leave
to cool. Make tea, strain and allow to cool, or use
strained cold tea from an earlier brew. Discard tea
leaves or bag. Rinse raisins in warm water. Chop or
mince raisins. Extract juice from lemons. Discard
pips, pith and peel. Pour red grape juice, lemon juice,
brewed tea, and dissolved sugar or honey into bucket.
Add raisins, wine yeast and cold water to raise the
total quantity of liquid to about 7 pints (4 litres).
Allow at least 2 inches (51mm) – 4 inches (102mm)
at the top of your bucket for the fermentation's initial
frothing. Cover. Keep bucket in a warm place for 7
days. Stir twice daily.

After seven days pour or scoop the fermenting wine
from its sediment and strain into a narrow-necked
1 gallon (4½ litres) fermentation vessel. Discard solids.
Top up to the neck with cold water. Fit cork or rubber
bung and air lock filled with water, or sulphite solution (see page 39). Leave in the warm until fermen-

tation is complete; this can take 4–5 weeks at an even temperature of 18°C (64°F).

Fermentation has finished when bubbles have ceased passing through the liquid in the air lock. A wine hydrometer reading (see page 44) of around 0.997 indicates fermentation may have ended. Check your thyme herb wine tastes dry (non-sweet), is not fizzy on your tongue and is beginning to fall clear from the surface downwards.

When satisfied fermentation has finished, syphon or pour wine from its sediment into a narrow-necked 1 gallon (4½ litres) storage vessel. Top up to the neck with wine of a similar flavour and colour, or cold water. Fit a cork or rubber bung. Store somewhere cool to clear and mature before bottling.

Your thyme herb wine should be clear and ready to bottle after about 7 months' storage, though a few months longer improves the wine's quality. When bottled, the wine needs a further 2–3 months to condition and mature before drinking.

Thyme herb wine achieves peak excellence about 22 months after the fermented wine has been transferred to a storage vessel to clear and mature.

THYME DARK-RUM LIQUEUR

Thyme dark-rum liqueur is a flame-amber colour, with rich fragrance and heart-warming flavour. Alcoholic strength (when dark-rum of around 40% Vol is used) about 23% alcohol by volume. Stronger dark-rum produces a more potent liqueur!

*Dried thyme leaves, spices, pure juice and honeys are available from your local health-food stockist.

INGREDIENTS: to make 1 standard-size wine bottle.
Fresh thyme leaves – ½ pint (284ml)
  or *dried leaves – ½ oz (14g)
*Pure orange juice – 6 fl oz (170ml)
*Pure orange blossom or lime blossom honey, or
  thyme honey – 4 heaped tablespoons
Coriander (ground) – ¼ level 5ml teaspoon
Mace (ground) – ¼ level 5ml teaspoon
Clove (whole) – 1
Dark rum – 17 fl oz (483ml)

Large jar (with tight-fitting lid) – big enough to hold
all ingredients, or one empty 1 litre wine, spirit or
cider bottle (in which to macerate ingredients) and
cork or plastic stopper.

METHOD

Sterilise (see page 38) and *rinse* utensils before use.
To measure fresh thyme leaves (if used), remove and
discard pieces of stalk and gently press leaves in
measuring jug. Lightly rinse fresh leaves in cold
water. Warm orange juice in small saucepan. Stir in
honey, coriander and mace. When dissolved, cover
and allow to cool. Place thyme leaves, clove, then
dark-rum and lastly juice-honey mixture in jar or
bottle (use a plastic funnel for liquid). Fasten lid or
stopper. Store somewhere warm for 10 days. Then
strain liqueur through a fine-mesh strainer into a large
jug. Squeeze liquid from leaves. Discard solids. Pour
the cloudy liqueur through a plastic funnel into an
empty wine bottle. Stopper the bottle with a cork or
plastic stopper. Store in a cool place for 9 weeks to
clear and permit the flavours to blend and mellow.
Then syphon or carefully pour the liqueur from its
sediment into a large jug; filter (see page 50) liqueur

through a plastic funnel into an empty wine or liqueur bottle – fasten a cork or plastic stopper.

Your Thyme Dark-Rum Liqueur is now ready to enjoy, and should continue to improve in quality for a further 9–12 weeks, before achieving peak excellence. Serve at room temperature in liqueur glasses. Good health!

Sweet Violet

VIOLET, SWEET *(Viola odorata)*.

The shade-seeking "shrinking violet" has always been a symbol of modesty. The beautiful and fragrant sweet violet, with its heart-shaped leaves, is linked with love and romance.

The Athenians adopted the violet as the floral emblem of ancient Athens. The flower – sacred to Aphrodite (Venus) goddess of beauty, love and fertility – was believed to help change bad luck and bring good fortune. The sweet violet was greatly valued for its healing power and culinary uses.

The sweet violet's flowers flavour commercial liqueurs (including Amourette, Crème De Violette, and Crème Yvette); they are candied and eaten as sweets, and used to decorate cakes, and biscuits and to flavour puddings. The flowers and/or leaves are an appetising addition to salad and sandwiches!

The flowers also make a delicious honey-syrup. Oil extracted from the petals is used in high quality French perfumes.

Sweet violet is a perennial plant of around 6 inches (0.15m) in height. It likes moist, partially shaded soil in a sheltered position – it grows in meadows, woods and hedgerows; and is also a popular ornamental plant in gardens. Sweet violet's mainly mauve-pink-violet (sometimes white) flowers bloom from March to April.

Parts used for liqueur: Flowers (best picked after dew has dried from petals, and before afternoon sunshine evaporates the flowers' natural oils).

SWEET VIOLET LIQUEUR

Sweet violet liqueur develops a lovely red-gold colour, with sweet fragrance and glorious, stimulating taste. Alcoholic strength (when brandy of around 40% Vol is used) about 23% alcohol by volume. Stronger brandy produces a more potent liqueur!

*Dried sweet violet flowers, spices, pure juice and honeys are available from your local health-food stockist.

INGREDIENTS: to make 1 standard-size wine bottle.
Fresh sweet violet flowers – ½ pint (284ml)
  or *dried flowers – ½ oz (14g)
***Pure red grape juice – 6 fl oz (170ml)**
***Pure orange blossom or lime blossom honey –**
  4 heaped tablespoons
Cinnamon (ground) – ¼ level 5ml teaspoon
Mace (ground) – ¼ level 5ml teaspoon
Nutmeg (ground) – ¼ level 5ml teaspoon
Pure lemon juice – 2 level 5ml teaspoons
Brandy – 17 fl oz (483ml)

**Large jar (with tight-fitting lid) – big enough to hold
all ingredients, or one empty 1 litre wine, spirit or
cider bottle (in which to macerate ingredients) and
cork or plastic stopper.**

METHOD
  Sterilise (see page 38) and *rinse* utensils before use.
To measure fresh sweet violet flowers (if used),
remove and discard pieces of green leaf and stalk and
gently press fresh flowers in measuring jug. Lightly
rinse fresh sweet violet flowers in cold water. Warm
grape juice in small saucepan. Stir in honey, cinnamon, mace, nutmeg and lemon juice. When dissolved, cover and allow to cool. Place sweet violet
flowers, then brandy and lastly juice-honey mixture
in jar or bottle (use a plastic funnel for liquid). Fasten
lid or stopper. Store somewhere warm for 10 days.
Then strain liqueur through a fine-mesh strainer into
a large jug. Squeeze liquid from flowers. Discard
solids. Pour the cloudy liqueur through a plastic funnel into an empty wine bottle. Stopper the bottle with
a cork or plastic stopper. Store in a cool place for 9
weeks to clear and permit the flavours to blend and

mellow. Then syphon or carefully pour the liqueur from its sediment into a large jug; filter (see page 50) liqueur through a plastic funnel into an empty wine or liqueur bottle – fasten a cork or plastic stopper.

Your Sweet Violet Liqueur is now ready to enjoy, and should continue to improve in quality for a further 9–12 weeks, before achieving peak excellence. Serve at room temperature in liqueur glasses. Good health!

Woodruff

WOODRUFF *(Galium odoratum;* also known as *Asperula odorata).*

Woodruff leaves, after being dried, become extraordinarily fragrant and imbue drinks with their uniquely delicious scent and taste. Dried woodruff leaves flavour traditional country wines, ales, fruit juice drinks, herbal tea and party punches. Dried leaves are used to flavour commercial liqueurs; and also in the manufacture of perfumes.

Woodruff is a perennial plant of around 8 inches (0.23m) in height. It likes moist soil in a shaded position. Woodruff's white flowers bloom from April to June.

● Woodruff grows well indoors.

Parts used for wine: Leaves (best gathered from May to July). Remove and discard pieces of stalk; dry fresh leaves in a warm place (see page 29) before use. 5 oz (142g) of fresh leaves dry to about 1 oz (28g).

WOODRUFF HERB WINE

Woodruff herb wine develops a light yellow-gold colour, with sweet fragrance and refreshing taste; enjoyable as an aperitif, table or social wine of about 12.5% alcohol by volume.

Sultanas (dried white grapes) give extra flavour, body and smoothness to this wine and nourish the wine yeast, encouraging maximum efficiency in alcohol production.

*Dried herbs, pure juices and honeys are available from your local health-food stockist.

INGREDIENTS: to make 1 gallon (4½ litres).
*Dried woodruff leaves – 1 oz (28g)
Water – up to 1 gallon (4½ litres)
Granulated sugar *(optional, see below)* **– 1½ lb (680g)**
Tea, strong – ½ cup
Sultanas – 12 oz (340g)
Lemons – 2
*Pure white grape juice – 1¾ pints (1 litre)
Wine yeast – amount recommended by manufacturer

SUGAR-FREE "SECRET" RECIPE (see page 23): To make woodruff herb wine without adding sugar (sucrose) replace the entire quantity of granulated sugar with **1 lb (454g)** of ***pure acacia blossom or mixed blossom honey**; and either **2¾ pints (1½ litres)** of ***pure white grape juice**, or **¾ pint (426ml)** of **wine making concentrated white grape juice.**

METHOD
Sterilise (see page 38) and *rinse* wine making equipment and utensils before use. Put dried leaves in plastic (food grade) bucket. Cover. Warm 1 pint

(½ litre) of water in large saucepan. Stir in granulated sugar or pure honey. When dissolved, cover and leave to cool. Make tea, strain and allow to cool, or use strained cold tea from an earlier brew. Discard tea leaves or bag. Rinse sultanas in warm water. Chop or mince sultanas. Extract juice from lemons. Discard pips, pith and peel. Pour white grape juice, lemon juice, brewed tea, and dissolved sugar or honey into bucket. Add sultanas, wine yeast and cold water to raise the total quantity of liquid to about 7 pints (4 litres). Allow at least 2 inches (51mm) – 4 inches (102mm) at the top of your bucket for the fermentation's initial frothing. Cover. Keep bucket in a warm place for 7 days. Stir twice daily.

After seven days pour or scoop the fermenting wine from its sediment and strain into a narrow-necked 1 gallon (4½ litres) fermentation vessel. Discard solids. Top up to the neck with cold water. Fit cork or rubber bung and air lock filled with water, or sulphite solution (see page 39). Leave in the warm until fermentation is complete; this can take 4–5 weeks at an even temperature of 18°C (64°F).

Fermentation has finished when bubbles have ceased passing through the liquid in the air lock. A wine hydrometer reading (see page 44) of around 0.997 indicates fermentation may have ended. Check your woodruff herb wine tastes dry (non-sweet), is not fizzy on your tongue and is beginning to fall clear from the surface downwards.

When satisfied fermentation has finished, syphon or pour wine from its sediment into a narrow-necked 1 gallon (4½ litres) storage vessel. Top up to the neck with wine of a similar flavour and colour, or cold water. Fit a cork or rubber bung. Store somewhere cool to clear and mature before bottling.

Your woodruff herb wine should be clear and ready to bottle after about 6 months' storage, though a few months longer improves the wine's quality. When bottled, the wine needs a further 2–3 months to condition and mature before drinking.

Woodruff herb wine achieves peak excellence about 20 months after the fermented wine has been transferred to a storage vessel to clear and mature.

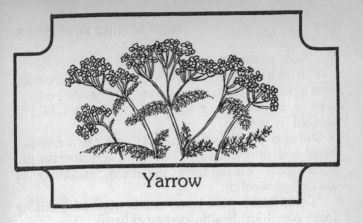

Yarrow

YARROW *(Achillea millefolium).*

Yarrow is a popular ingredient for making traditional country wine, ale and herbal tea. Yarrow's spicy-bitter leaves can be enjoyed (in moderation) with salad; and also as a cooked vegetable.

According to folklore, yarrow wine increases psychic sensitivity. Dried yarrow stalks are used in the ritual when consulting the ancient and respected Chinese oracle – "I Ching" *(Book of Changes).*

Yarrow is a perennial plant of around 15 inches (0.38m) in height; it likes well-drained soil in a sunny position, and grows wild in grassy places. Yarrow's grey-white or pink flowers bloom from June to November.

Parts used for wine and liqueur: Leaves (best gathered from June to September). Yarrow flowers may be used in addition to leaves, bestowing extra aroma, colour (pink flowers especially) and flavour to yarrow wine or liqueur. Add 2 level *table*spoons of fresh flowers, or 1 level *table*spoon of dried flowers to either the herb wine or liqueur recipe. Any such addition is optional, and left to your discretion.

YARROW HERB WINE

Yarrow herb (leaf) wine develops an amber colour, with a pleasing aroma and warm spicy flavour; enjoyable as an aperitif or social wine of about 11.5% alcohol by volume.

Sultanas (dried white grapes) give extra flavour, body and smoothness to this wine and nourish the wine yeast, encouraging maximum efficiency in alcohol production.

*Dried herbs, pure juices and honeys are available from your local health-food stockist.

INGREDIENTS: to make 1 gallon (4½ litres).
Fresh yarrow leaves – 1 pint (½ litre)
    or *dried leaves – 1 oz (28g)
Water – up to 1 gallon (4½ litres)
Granulated sugar *(optional, see below)* **– 1½ lb (680g)**
Tea, strong – ½ cup
Sultanas – 12 oz (340g)
***Pure orange juice – 1¾ pints (1 litre)**
Wine yeast – amount recommended by manufacturer

SUGAR-FREE "SECRET" RECIPE (see page 23): To make yarrow herb wine without adding sugar (sucrose) replace the entire quantity of granulated sugar with **1 lb (454g)** of *pure orange blossom or lime blossom honey; and either **2¾ pints (1½ litres)** of *pure white grape juice, or **¾ pint (426ml)** of wine making concentrated white grape juice.

METHOD

Sterilise (see page 38) and *rinse* wine making equipment and utensils before use. To measure fresh yarrow leaves (if used), discard pieces of stripped stalk and gently press leaves in measuring jug. Lightly rinse fresh leaves in cold water. Put fresh or dried leaves in plastic (food grade) bucket. Cover. Warm 1 pint (½ litre) of water in large saucepan. Stir in granulated sugar or pure honey. When dissolved, cover and leave to cool. Make tea, strain and allow to cool, or use strained cold tea from an earlier brew. Discard tea leaves or bag. Rinse sultanas in warm water. Chop or mince sultanas. Pour pure orange juice, and grape juice (if used), brewed tea, and dissolved sugar or honey into bucket. Add sultanas, wine yeast and cold water to raise the total quantity of liquid to about 7 pints (4 litres). Allow at least 2 inches (51mm) – 4 inches (102mm) at the top of your bucket for the fermentation's initial frothing. Cover. Keep bucket in a warm place for 7 days. Stir twice daily.

After seven days pour or scoop the fermenting wine from its sediment and strain into a narrow-necked 1 gallon (4½ litres) fermentation vessel. Discard solids. Top up to the neck with cold water. Fit cork or rubber bung and air lock filled with water, or sulphite solution (see page 39). Leave in the warm until fermentation is complete; this can take 4–5 weeks at an even temperature of 18°C (64°F).

Fermentation has finished when bubbles have ceased passing through the liquid in the air lock. A wine hydrometer reading (see page 44) of around 0.997 indicates fermentation may have ended. Check your yarrow herb wine tastes dry (non-sweet), is not fizzy on your tongue and is beginning to fall clear from the surface downwards.

When satisfied fermentation has finished, syphon or pour wine from its sediment into a narrow-necked 1 gallon (4½ litres) storage vessel. Top up to the neck with wine of a similar flavour and colour, or cold water. Fit a cork or rubber bung. Store somewhere cool to clear and mature before bottling.

Your yarrow herb wine should be clear and ready to bottle after about 6 months' storage, though a few months longer improves the wine's quality. When bottled, the wine needs a further 2–3 months to condition and mature before drinking.

Yarrow herb wine achieves peak excellence about 20 months after the fermented wine has been transferred to a storage vessel to clear and mature.

YARROW WHISKY LIQUEUR

Yarrow whisky liqueur shines a bright gold colour, with a splendid aroma and hot spicy flavour; a friendly drink to brighten wintry evenings – my favourite cold cure. Alcoholic strength (when whisky of around 40% Vol is used) about 23% alcohol by volume. Stronger whisky produces a more potent liqueur!

*Dried yarrow leaves, spices, pure juice and honeys are available from your local health-food stockist.

INGREDIENTS: to make 1 standard-size wine bottle.
Fresh yarrow leaves – ½ pint (284ml)
 or *dried leaves – ½ oz (14g)
*Pure apple juice – 6 fl oz (170ml)
*Pure acacia blossom or mixed blossom honey –
 4 heaped tablespoons
Ginger (ground) – ½ level 5ml teaspoon
Pure lemon juice – 2 level 5ml teaspoons
Scotch Whisky or Irish Whiskey – 17 fl oz (483ml)

Large jar (with tight-fitting lid) – big enough to hold all ingredients, or one empty 1 litre wine, spirit or cider bottle (in which to macerate ingredients) and cork or plastic stopper.

METHOD

Sterilise (see page 38) and *rinse* utensils before use. To measure fresh yarrow leaves (if used), remove and discard pieces of stalk and gently press leaves in measuring jug. Lightly rinse fresh leaves in cold water. Warm apple juice in small saucepan. Stir in honey, ginger and lemon juice. When dissolved, cover and allow to cool. Place yarrow leaves, then whisky and lastly juice-honey mixture in jar or bottle (use a plastic funnel for liquid). Fasten lid or stopper. Store somewhere warm for 10 days. Then strain liqueur through a fine-mesh strainer into a large jug. Squeeze liquid from leaves. Discard solids. Pour the cloudy liqueur through a plastic funnel into an empty wine bottle. Stopper the bottle with a cork or plastic stopper. Store in a cool place for 9 weeks to clear and permit the flavours to blend and mellow. Then syphon or carefully pour the liqueur from its sediment into a large jug; filter (see page 50) liqueur through a plastic funnel into an empty wine or liqueur bottle – fasten a cork or plastic stopper.

Your Yarrow Whisky Liqueur is now ready to enjoy, and should continue to improve in quality for a further 9–12 weeks, before achieving peak excellence. Serve at room temperature in liqueur glasses. Good health!

THE ELIXIR OF LIFE

The quest by medieval alchemists for a herbal elixir of life, to slow the body's natural ageing process, and bless us with prolonged youth and vigour, resulted in many complex herb liqueur recipes. My own simple version, which is distilled from several of the more popular medieval alchemical formulas, is detailed below. In fairness, I should mention that the original recipes emphasise the importance to sustained youthfulness and longevity of a vegetarian diet, fresh air and regular exercise, and a peaceful, religious-spiritual, happy and contented way of life – free from needless worry!

An *occasional* liqueur glass of the elixir is recommended – moderation in all things. After all, who wants to live forever . . .!?

Herbs used for the elixir: Balm leaves (see page 62); Rose petals (see page 148); Rosemary leaves (see page 154), and Sage leaves (see page 158).

THE ELIXIR OF LIFE

The Elixir of Life is a distinctive gold-red colour, with exotic fragrance and exciting flavour. Alcoholic strength (when brandy of around 40% Vol is used) about 23% alcohol by volume. Stronger brandy produces a more potent elixir!

*Dried balm leaves, rose petals, rosemary leaves, sage leaves, spices, pure juice and honeys are available from your local health-food stockist. Dried rose petals are also available from home-brew stockists.

INGREDIENTS: to make 1 standard-size wine bottle.
*Pure red grape juice – 6 fl oz (170ml)
*Pure acacia blossom or lime blossom honey –
   4 heaped tablespoons
Ginger (ground) – ½ level 5ml teaspoon
Nutmeg (ground) – ¼ level 5ml teaspoon
Pure lemon juice – 2 level 5ml teaspoons
Fresh balm leaves – ¼ pint (142ml)
   or *dried leaves – ¼ oz (7g)
Fresh rose petals (single or mixed colours) – ¼ pint
   (142ml) or *dried petals – ¼ oz (7g)
Fresh rosemary leaves – 1 heaped 5ml teaspoon
   or *dried leaves – 1 level 5ml teaspoon
Fresh sage leaves – 1 heaped tablespoon
   or *dried leaves – 1 level tablespoon
Brandy – 17 fl oz (483ml)

Large jar (with tight-fitting lid) – big enough to hold
all ingredients, or one empty 1 litre wine, spirit or cider
bottle (in which to macerate ingredients) and cork or
plastic stopper.

METHOD
   Sterilise (see page 38) and *rinse* utensils before use.
Warm grape juice in small saucepan. Stir in honey,
ginger, nutmeg and lemon juice. When dissolved,
cover and allow to cool. Lightly rinse fresh herbs (if
used), in cold water. Place balm leaves, rose petals,
rosemary leaves and sage leaves, then brandy and
lastly juice-honey mixture in jar or bottle (use a plastic
funnel for liquid). Fasten lid or stopper. Store somewhere warm for 10 days. Then strain elixir through
a plastic funnel into an empty wine bottle. Stopper
the bottle with a cork or plastic stopper. Store in a
cool place for 12 weeks to clear and permit the

flavours to blend and mellow. Then syphon or carefully pour the liqueur from its sediment into a large jug; filter (see page 50) elixir through a plastic funnel into an empty wine or liqueur bottle – fasten a cork or plastic stopper.

The Elixir of Life is now ready to enjoy, and should continue to improve in quality for a further 9–12 weeks, before achieving peak excellence. Serve at room temperature in liqueur glasses. Best wishes for good health and a long and happy life. Cheers!

Index

OTHER WINEMAKING PAPERFRONTS

Also by Ian Ball

WINE MAKING THE NATURAL WAY

As its title suggests, this book concentrates on making wine from natural ingredients, without using chemical additives. Wholesome fruits, flowers, vegetables, etc., are free for gathering or can be bought in season while prices are low. Using them as close to their original form as possible safeguards healing properties and retains valuable oils and scents while maximum flavour, vitamins and goodness are extracted. Each recipe also includes details of how to make *sugar-free* wines.

TRADITIONAL BEER & CIDER MAKING

Ian Ball revives many of the traditional brews enjoyed by our forebears. He gives recipes for a wide selection of types of beer, ale, lager and stout; all of which can be made from *natural ingredients without added chemicals*, and can be bottled or barrelled at home and ready for drinking within a few weeks. As minimal equipment is needed, the finest pint will cost you only a fraction of the price you would pay over the bar.

The second part of the book shows how you, at home, can revive the ancient craft of cider making, and provide enjoyment for your family and friends.

Each uniform with this book

ELLIOT RIGHT WAY BOOKS, KINGSWOOD, SURREY, U.K.

OTHER WINEMAKING PAPERFRONTS

HOME WINE MAKING THE RIGHT WAY

Kenneth Hawkins reveals the secrets of successful home winemaking, having 20 years' experience and many awards to his credit. He explains all the major elements of home winemaking, including a detailed analysis of how and why various types of wines differ and he shows how to train your palate to judge their relative qualities.

In fascinating asides to his 55 recipes, he delves into the customs, legends and stories which link individual wines to the celebration of special days and events.

EASY-MADE WINE & COUNTRY DRINKS

Mrs Gennery-Taylor's famous country recipes will bring lovely wines to your table for as little as a few pence per bottle. No expensive equipment is required, and the ingredients can be easily found in field and hedgerow.

Includes a clever wine calendar which tells you when to make each wine throughout the year.

Each uniform with this book

ELLIOT RIGHT WAY BOOKS, KINGSWOOD, SURREY, U.K.

OUR PUBLISHING POLICY

HOW WE CHOOSE

Our policy is to consider every deserving manuscript and we can give special editorial help where an author is an authority on his subject but an inexperienced writer. We are rigorously selective in the choice of books we publish. We set the highest standards of editorial quality and accuracy. This means that a *Paperfront* is easy to understand and delightful to read. Where illustrations are necessary to convey points of detail, these are drawn up by a subject specialist artist from our panel.

HOW WE KEEP PRICES LOW

We aim for the big seller. This enables us to order enormous print runs and achieve the lowest price for you. Unfortunately, this means that you will not find in the *Paperfront* list any titles on obscure subjects of minority interest only. These could not be printed in large enough quantities to be sold for the low price at which we offer this series.

We sell almost all our *Paperfronts* at the same unit price. This saves a lot of fiddling about in our clerical departments and helps us to give you world-beating value. Under this system, the longer titles are offered at a price which we believe to be unmatched by any publisher in the world.

OUR DISTRIBUTION SYSTEM

Because of the competitive price, and the rapid turnover, *Paperfronts* are possibly the most profitable line a bookseller can handle. They are stocked by the best bookshops all over the world. It may be that your bookseller has run out of stock of a particular title. If so, he can order more from us at any time – we have a fine reputation for "same day" despatch, and we supply any order, however small (even a single copy), to any bookseller who has an account with us. We prefer you to buy from your bookseller, as this reminds him of the strong underlying public demand for *Paperfronts*. Members of the public who live in remote places, or who are housebound, or whose local bookseller is unco-operative, can order direct from us by post.

FREE

If you would like an up-to-date list of all paperfront titles currently available, send a stamped self-addressed envelope to
ELLIOT RIGHT WAY BOOKS, BRIGHTON RD.,
LOWER KINGSWOOD, SURREY, U.K.